D1594062

LIFE BEYOND SHOULD

OVERCOME EXPECTATIONS &
CREATE THE LIFE YOU WANT

VICKI MOORE

NEW DEGREE PRESS

COPYRIGHT © 2021 VICKI MOORE
All rights reserved.

LIFE BEYOND SHOULD
Overcome Expectations & Create the Life You Want

ISBN   978-1-63676-808-3   *Paperback*
          978-1-63730-234-7   *Kindle Ebook*
          978-1-63730-251-4   *Ebook*

"To be yourself in a world that is constantly trying to make you something else is the greatest accomplishment."

- RALPH WALDO EMERSON

CONTENTS

———

INTRODUCTION

———

"As I find myself looking out from the 45th floor, I reflect on how wrong my definition of success was."[1]

That was what Alexandra Galviz posted on LinkedIn on her last day at the prestigious financial exchange company where she worked. She had resigned from her job without knowing what would come next.

Alex was a woman on a mission from a young age. She had set ambitious goals for herself. While still in university, she had decided that by thirty she would have "an executive leadership role at a firm in the city, with international travel, expensive clothes, and the lifestyle of success."

At twenty-four, she had already achieved her goals, or at least what she thought were her goals. She had also suffered two burnouts, accumulated significant debt, and could barely drag herself to work each day in the luxurious office building

———

1   Alexandra Galviz (Authentic Alex), "When I was a little girl, I used to secretly dream of working in that really tall building with the pointy top...," LinkedIn, February, 2017.

at Canary Wharf overlooking London. Alex had attained incredible success, but at what cost?

As she captured in her post, "Society, media, family, peers, lead us to believe that success is money, status, and power. What they fail to explain is that it comes at a price (burnout, stress, broken relationships, to name a few.)"[2] The breaking point for Alex finally came when her company offered her a promotion. Instead of being elated, she felt deflated. The thought of having even more responsibility and more of *this* life, the one she thought she had wanted, was more than she could bear. On the surface, her life looked perfect, even enviable, but she was miserable and felt lost.

She recalls thinking, "What am I doing with my life?"

When she answered her own question with, "I help salespeople sell better to make rich people richer," she realized that her job was not aligned with her values.

Instead of accepting the promotion, she made the decision to leave her job, but she didn't have a plan. She had spent so much time molding herself to the demands and expectations of other people in the high-pressure, male-dominated industry that she no longer knew what to expect of herself.

As she left her corporate career that day, the final sentence of her farewell post summed up her experience. "Sometimes

---

2   Ibid.

it takes getting to where you want to be to realize it is not where you are meant to be."[3]

Now, three years later, Alex has completely reinvented both her personal and professional life to align with her values—helping people to find their purpose, deal with trauma, and express themselves authentically.

I connected with Alex because we had similar roles in training and development, and her story of stress and overwhelm felt very familiar. We each had a passion for our work but also felt compelled to leave it at the peak of our success. As we talked about her experience, I wondered why so many people need to hit rock bottom or be on the verge of a breakdown in order to choose a different path. Too many times, the clients I talk with are burnt out, stressed out, and are losing hope that it will ever get better. They feel stuck on a hamster wheel, and they aren't exactly sure how they got onto it in the first place.

* * *

When I ask why they don't make a change, the answer almost always includes the same word: *should*. They created their life the way everyone said they *should*. They followed all the right steps in the formula to achieve success and happiness. Changing the formula, taking a risk, and doing it differently seemed somehow irresponsible, reserved for people who are the exception.

---

3   Ibid.

When I was growing up, the formula went something like this:

Get a good education + find a good job + work hard + get married + follow the proven path = you'll have a great life and live happily ever after.

Today, it sounds little different, but it is basically the same:

Anything is possible. You can have it all. You can hack your life to achieve mega-success and instant happiness. Whatever it is, there's an app for that.

It sounds a lot sexier and more exciting now, but it boils down to the same message—follow the prescribed formula, and you'll have a happy, successful life. It seems straightforward enough, and there is certainly no shortage of advice on how to do it. A simple Google search on the word "hacks" returns over one trillion results.

In our relentless pursuit of success and happiness, we have somehow achieved exactly the opposite. Despite, or perhaps because of, the incredible volume and ease of access to information, we are becoming more and more miserable.

There is a growing portion of the population experiencing Impostor Syndrome and burnout.[4] Either we don't believe we are capable of succeeding, or we work ourselves into a health crisis just to prove we are good enough.

---

4   Jayne Leonard, "How to Handle Impostor Syndrome," *Medical News Today*, September 29, 2020.

Consider what recent studies are telling us about how satisfied, or dissatisfied, we are with work and life:

- A Gallup survey in 2019 reported that two-thirds of Americans feel burnt out at some time.[5]
- Recent research shows that, around the world, negative feelings such as worry, sadness, and anger are increasing, up by 27 percent from 2010 to 2018.[6]
- In the United States, overall happiness has been steadily declining since 2011, after reaching a peak in the 1990s.[7]

If more resources than ever before are readily available to us, and we have an endless supply of easy-to-follow checklists for success, why are more and more people feeling so stuck, worried, overwhelmed, and unhappy? Maybe doing what we *should* do is not the best path to fulfillment, success, and happiness.

Perhaps the best formula for a happy, successful life is actually not to follow a formula at all.

Pursuing something that is out of alignment with our talents and desires requires much more effort to achieve only average results. In these instances, even if we are driven and committed enough to achieve extraordinary success, we

---

5   Ben Wigert and Sangeeta Agrawal, "Employee Burnout: Part 1," *Gallup*, July 12, 2018.

6   Kira Newman, "World Happiness Report Finds that People are Feeling Worse," *Greater Good Magazine*, March 20, 2019.

7   John F. Helliwell, Richard Layard and Jeffrey D. Sachs, *World Happiness Report 2019* (New York: Sustainable Development Solutions Network, 2019), chap. 5.

often sacrifice much along the way, including health, relationships, and personal goals. Without these, it becomes a hollow victory.

The good news is that there is a different way. It is possible to achieve your personal version of success and do it in a way that is aligned with your unique talents and desires. The people who achieve exceptional results are people that have somehow recognized this early in their lives. Rather than following the defined formula for success, they follow their own path, pursue their own ideas, and live their own lives unapologetically. They are the exception.

* * *

I too fell into the trap of doing all the "right things" early in my life. I started my career in marketing and quickly advanced to managing teams and large agency accounts with clients like Toyota and Honda. As an ambitious woman in a high-pressure industry, I worked incredibly long hours and lived by the motto, "I'll sleep enough when I am dead." At the pace I was going, that possibility wasn't very far into the future. Sixteen-hour workdays, Red Bull for breakfast, and sleeping on the couch in the office lobby were not uncommon.

Luckily, I didn't need to hit rock-bottom in order to see that I was on the wrong path. Two health scares were enough to get my attention. After one particularly intense new product launch, a routine check-up revealed heart palpitations. Only a few months later, a stress-related illness put me at risk of losing my vision. For months, I had to wear dark sunglasses at my desk and could barely see my computer. That forced me to change the way I worked. To my surprise, I was able to work fewer hours and earn more money, simply by taking a different approach. My career continued to grow and offer greater opportunities, but I still felt something was missing.

When I gave up everything in 2014 to pursue my dream of living in Europe, everyone told me how brave I was. They saw it as a huge risk to quit my job, sell all of my belongings, and relocate to a country where I didn't speak the language, didn't have a job, and knew no one. But I never felt brave. For me, continuing to stay stuck in the "safe" life everyone expected me to lead seemed much riskier than pursuing the life I actually wanted.

It wasn't easy. In fact, it is one of the hardest things I have ever done. Aside from leaving my friends and having absolutely no support system, I was also learning everything again as if I was a child. As a successful corporate executive, who took pride in being able to solve complex problems, my ego took a huge blow. Suddenly, I realized that I didn't know how to open a bank account, pay my electric bill, or even buy groceries in the country that was now my home.

My lack of confidence and the struggle to accomplish daily tasks was made worse by all of the people I met who couldn't understand. Why would I give up a successful career and life at the beach in Southern California to move to Germany? Every conversation started with the same question, "But why would you do *that*?" Somehow the answer, "Because I always wanted to live in Europe," seemed pathetically insufficient.

Ultimately, it was worth every tear, every lonely night, and every moment of struggle.

Now when people talk to me, they no longer question if I've lost my sanity. Instead, the conversation has changed to, "I wish I could do that, but..." or "I wish that were possible for me..." Those opening phrases are then quickly followed by all the reasons these choices aren't available for them.

They see me as the exception.

I know that I am not, because I hear stories every day from people in all sorts of circumstances who have taken the risk to create their own formula for success and happiness.

* * *

It is not our fault that we don't realize how exceptional we are. We are trained from an early age to meet the expectations of other people—parents, teachers, society. We are taught to follow the rules, look a certain way, and behave and think according to the norms. Creativity is quickly replaced by memorizing school subjects and pursuing good grades. Being the exception at a young age often means being a misfit and results in being teased or bullied. As we get older, we carry the pressure to conform with us into our work and personal lives.

My theory is that the more information we have at our fingertips and the more possibilities we have available, the less likely we are to be confident in expressing our own unique ideas. You can now Google anything from how to build a website to how to build a house. This digital information overload results in two problems. First, we no longer need to be resourceful or creative, and thus, we stop thinking for ourselves. Second, we begin to doubt ourselves in everything we do. If anyone can watch a video about how to start an online business, and we somehow manage to do it wrong, we must be a total failure.

Before the internet (yes, there was a time, long, long ago and far away), we only compared ourselves to the people in our schools or in our neighborhoods. Now, we can compare ourselves instantly and constantly to everyone in the world. "Keeping up with the Joneses" is simply overwhelming. We achieve more and more and yet are less and less fulfilled and satisfied. And the phenomenon is growing.

We are bombarded from all directions with so much information about what we *should* do that we never slow down long enough to think about what we truly *want* to do. The truth is, whether we realize it or not, we are still making that choice. We put ourselves on the hamster wheel of *should,* and only we can jump off of it.

My hope is that this book might help to show that it doesn't require a crisis to jump off the hamster wheel. You have the option to pursue what you want rather than what others think you *should* want. And it is much easier to jump off the wheel before it is on fire.

We are not meant to do exactly what everyone else does. We are each unique, not only genetically but also in our thoughts and experiences. Each person has different aspirations and values, supported by individual talents, gifts, and perspectives. Now more than ever, the world needs these unique contributions.

I believe the people we consider exceptional are ordinary people who do something differently to create extraordinary results, and that we all have the power to be exceptional.

WHY READ THIS BOOK

If you are looking for life hacks to help you make billions of dollars, create a successful start-up, or get a million followers on the latest social media channel, you've got the wrong book. I haven't done any of those things, and those books have already been written.

This book is for people who are ready to unhack their lives, stop feeling trapped in the spiral of expectations, get unstuck, and start living the life they truly want to live.

Perhaps you are at the early stages of your career and already overwhelmed by the expectations of your boss and your colleagues, not to mention the pressure to keep up a social life and "have it all." Or maybe you've built a pretty good life, at least on the surface. You are successful in your career, have a nice house and an expensive car, and take holidays that look good on Instagram. You've achieved your goals but still somehow feel unfulfilled.

This book shares the stories and strategies of people who took a different approach. These are regular people who have become the exception using strategies that you too can apply.

Some of them you may already know about. They include actors, authors, and CEOs of world-changing companies. But there are also those whom you may not have heard about. They include people like:

- The corporate executive who gave up his high-salary career to lead a nonprofit humanitarian organization, working to make sure people around the world have clean drinking water
- The mother who started over as a student in her mid-forties, in order to create a new career that she loves and be the role model she wants her children to have
- The VP who left her career, changed her health, and pursued a business idea (now selling over $150 million) in an industry where she had zero experience, all based on an experiment in her kitchen

Whether they are celebrities, entrepreneurs, artists, or employees, all of these people have something in common. They didn't do what others expected of them or what they were told they *should* do. They had a vision for what they wanted, and they pursued it. They defined their own version of success and created their own strategy to get there.

In this book, you will learn the key strategies that helped these exceptional people change their lives in a wide variety of situations and at all ages. I discovered that their strategies include a specific type of courage that anyone can learn and apply.

In a world where we are continuously bombarded with what other people think, it is not always easy to find the courage to follow your own path. This book covers seven specific strategies, which will help you take control, choose the path that is right for you, and accelerate your ability to create the life you want. They are as much mindset as strategy, and young children seem to have them naturally. Sadly, as adults, we have lost sight of how useful they can be for creating a life that fills us with joy.

This book explores the seven components of this mindset of COURAGE, which helps people to create exceptional lives. If you watch a young child play for a day, you are likely to recognize every one of them.

Clarity of Purpose:	know what they want and why they want it
Overcome Expectations:	don't accept rules about how things are done and ask "why?"
Unapologetically Authentic:	act naturally as they are and don't worry about others' opinions
Return on Risk:	take risks and pursue their dreams (just ask a nurse how many kids have attempted to fly)
Accelerate Action:	take action toward their goals, rather than staying stuck in analysis
Grow through Challenge:	learn by doing and are not deterred by failure (when they fall, they get up, brush themselves off, and try again)
Embrace being Yourself:	believe they are capable of anything they choose

These strategies have the potential to transform everything from your daily activities to long-term results. They are based on concepts of behavioral science, but this book is not intended to be scientific advice, or any advice at all, for that matter. The ideas expressed in this book are based on my own experiences, interviews, and interpretations of available research. They are not intended to fully represent the complexities of the research and concepts referenced. I have attempted to use these concepts simply to offer a helpful framework and thought-provoking perspective.

I intend to show that we each have the potential to create a life perfectly suited for us. We only need to have the courage to embrace being the exception, believe in ourselves, and pursue our dreams.

LET'S GET STARTED

Before we jump right into the concept of COURAGE, we're going to take a look at a few of the things that make it difficult and how to recognize them. The book is written in two parts.

Part 1 takes a look at the influences in our lives that put us on the hamster wheel to begin with and how they keep us from leading an exceptional life. Understanding these influences will help you to challenge them and more easily mitigate the impact they have in your life.

Part 2 explores each of the components of courage in detail. You'll learn how each strategy impacts results through the stories of people that have used these concepts to powerfully change their lives.

Are you ready to start exploring what is possible, jump off of the wheel of expectations, and take control of creating the life that *you* want to live?

PART 1

THE STORY WE'VE BEEN TOLD

CHAPTER 1

LEADING AN EXCEPTIONAL LIFE

———

I'll never forget that day ten years ago. The most important person in my life had just told me I was average. At least that is what I heard during the conversation. It was simultaneously one of the most disappointing and one of the most motivating moments of my life. It became clear that day; the wonderful life I had spent years building was about to unravel completely.

Of course, it wasn't quite as blunt as that. The conversation had started simply enough. It was a beautiful, warm Saturday afternoon in Southern California. The dog enjoyed the sun on the front porch, and jazz music filled the room. My husband and I were doing a few chores around the new house we had moved into a few months earlier. We were excited to finally have a beautiful home, with a large office for my business, a big yard for the dog, and an open-plan kitchen well suited for entertaining friends. Everything seemed to be going perfectly. We had achieved all the major milestones and had started talking about our long-term plans.

My husband and I were fortunate enough to have many options available to us. His daughter would be going to college in a few years, and he would have a full pension and be able to take early retirement. I had a successful training business, which allowed me and my entire team to work remotely most of the time. I had always loved to travel. We got married on a cliff in Greece and spent our honeymoon running with the bulls in Spain. Sadly, the luxury of travel had been on hold for years, while my husband focused on his career and I built my business. Now, I was excited that travel could again be part of our lives.

I began, "In a few years, we won't be tied to jobs or schools, and we could start to travel more."

Apparently not as excited about the idea as I was, he replied, "Yeah, maybe."

I needed a new approach to the subject. Seven years earlier, during our honeymoon, we had fallen in love with the lifestyle, culture, and cuisine in Spain. We had both wished there was more time to explore and experience life there. I suggested, "We could even live in Spain for a year."

His reply had more energy this time but not the kind I had hoped for. "We can't do that," he said bluntly.

When I asked why, he immediately began listing the numerous reasons it wasn't possible. You would have thought I'd suggested that we live on Mars. I had talked with friends who had spent several years living abroad with their children. I had also done some research after hearing their stories and experiences and how they made it possible. I tried again, with real-life examples of people he knew, "People do it all the time. Scott and his wife went to South America for a year, even when they had small children. And we met people in Spain who moved there from Los Angeles with much less..."

He interrupted my examples, looked at me and said, "Those are the exceptions."

Well, that quickly shut down the conversation, and I took the dog for a walk. I felt numb, and I didn't really understand why until a few moments later. Then it hit me, the man I loved, the person who was supposed to believe in me the most, had just said that I was not exceptional. In his opinion, I was average, and I should be happy leading an average life.

Four years after that conversation, I moved to Europe, just as I had imagined. Everyone I met told me how brave I was for pursuing my dream and starting over—alone. I didn't understand what they meant. I didn't feel brave. But, in a way, they were right.

Since then, I have discovered something which sets people who lead exceptional lives apart, but it is probably not what you think.

We believe that people who succeed in pursuing their dream or passion are the exception. Whether they be actors, athletes, entrepreneurs, or executives, we are so focused on their accomplishments that we rarely take time to dig deeper and explore their path to success. We see the result, but we don't think about what contributed to achieving that outcome.

Most people assume that achieving exceptional results requires special talent or lots of luck, or some combination of the two. It turns out that it is usually neither, at least not by traditional definitions.

IT IS NOT TALENT

We believe that people who are most successful are especially intelligent or talented, but research has proven this is not the case. In his book, *Talent is Overrated*, Geoff Colvin explores the assumption that natural ability, or talent, is the distinguishing factor which results in world-class performance.[8] Instead, he finds that "intelligence and other general abilities play a much smaller role in top-level performance than most of us believe."[9] More often, research finds that high performers are relatively average people from normal circumstances who have worked incredibly hard to become extraordinary. Colvin states, "No one, not even the most 'talented' performers, became great without at least ten years of very hard preparation. If talent means that success is easy or rapid, as most people seem to believe,

---

8   Geoff Colvin, *Talent is Overrated: What Really Separates World-Class Performers from Everybody Else* (New York: Portfolio/Penguin, 2008), Kindle.

9   Colvin, *Talent is Overrated,* chap. 11.

then something is obviously wrong with a talent-based explanation of high achievement."[10]

Of course, talent and natural abilities are important to some extent. As a 5'3" woman, no matter how hard I work, I will never be a star basketball player. But as Colvin points out, natural abilities alone are not enough. Top performers do what Colvin refers to as "deliberate practice"—practicing in ways that are designed specifically to improve performance, with high repetition and continual feedback.[11] This consistent effort to improve results through focused practice is what separates great performers from good performers.

As I spoke with Darrian Douglas, a successful drummer and musician, he explained it this way: "to study theory is easy, but practice takes dedicated focus." He can't recall a day when he didn't practice for hours, sometimes up to eight hours per day.

Darrian knew at age three that he wanted to play the drums. Well, either that or be a Ninja Turtle. Darrian's father was a musician, and he was continually around music from a young age. He began his formal music education at age eleven, studying at the Academic and Performing Arts Center in Jackson, Mississippi. His teacher at the school, Dr. Perry Combs, secretly gave him drum lessons, because his mother had said "absolutely not" to this path of study.

---

10   Colvin, *Talent is Overrated,* chap. 4.
11   Ibid.

He continued to study the drums, now with his mother's permission, throughout school and into college. He told me, "I have played every day since I started. I have never not played." He built a successful career playing drums in New Orleans, New York, and at more than thirty music festivals around the world. But Darrian will be the first to tell you that it takes more than talent to achieve success. He now lives in New York City and explains it this way: "There is a small percentage of people playing at a very high level, and they are all competing for the same five gigs. It is like competing to be a starting player in the NBA. Most people, even though they are really talented, can't even get a chance to start."

Darrian got his chance to start by putting in an exceptional effort that others simply would not. He was booked every night at clubs in New Orleans, but he had always dreamed of moving to New York. He made the risky decision to move and pursue his music career there. No one in the city knew who he was and, with thousands of talented musicians there, he had to find a way to stand out.

New York is expensive, and he ran out of money within weeks after arriving. Just getting into a club cost more than forty dollars at the door, so he stood outside every night and listened through the windows. He recalls standing outside of a club at 96th and Broadway on a frigid December night in temperatures of 15°F. He would listen to a set and then go across the street to McDonald's to warm up before going back to hear the next set. Once Spring arrived, he carried his drums to Central Park every day at 5 a.m. in order to get a prime location. Then he waited there for five hours until the rest of the group arrived at 10 a.m. to start playing.

It took two years of struggling, but now Darrian plays at the clubs that he used to stand outside of. He has played at Carnegie Hall three times and tours around the world. There were times when he wanted to give up, but his girlfriend at the time encouraged him to keep going, telling him, "You didn't move to New York to get a job."

Darrian is still in the process of creating his success story, especially after the pandemic significantly impacted the music scene and opportunities to play. He sums it up this way: "Most people give up. If you don't give up, you are already ahead of the majority."

IT IS ALSO NOT LUCK

In the Spring of 2012, I was talking on the phone with my parents and trying to plan a family vacation, which is never an easy task. We discussed where we could go that would be both affordable and enjoyable for ten people. My father suggested that we go to the beach.

The next part of the conversation went like this:

Me: *I live at the beach.*

Dad: *Well, not all of us are that lucky.*

Mom: ***It's not luck; she planned it that way.***

My mother was referring to my decision fifteen years earlier to move cross-country from Virginia to the California coast. I had decided to pursue my dream of living in Los Angeles, without having a job or any contacts there at the time.

My father made the oversight that many people make when someone achieves a result they consider special, like a great job or a beautiful house on the beach. He was focused on the outcome, which was clear and visible each day, rather than what happened behind the scenes to obtain it. He had forgotten the part where I worked two jobs for over three years in order to save money. He overlooked the almost three-thousand-mile drive, which I made alone with only the belongings that fit in my car. And he forgot the part where I slept on the floor in three temporary apartments and had thirty-seven job interviews in less than three months before I achieved my goal.

We often assume that people who achieve amazing results somehow got a "lucky break," which is responsible for their success. We hear stories of a specific pivotal moment in their lives and then attribute their success to the luck of that one event.

It is easy and exciting to focus on the moment when things took a turn.

If you dig a bit deeper, you discover that they created the situation in which the pivotal "lucky" moment became possible. Often, like Darrian, they worked for months or years, sacrificing other opportunities, in order to be in the right place at the right time. They passed up safer or more predictable options, risked their savings, and overcame difficulties to pursue their goal. They took action which ensured that they were available and prepared for the lucky break when it happened.

In other words, they planned it that way.

In Darrian's case, many people would consider it a lucky break that he was invited to play with a well-known jazz musician, Ellis Marsalis, at a New Orleans club when he was only twenty. I asked him how he happened to get such a great opportunity. He explained, "I had been driving one and a half hours to New Orleans every weekend to hang out at this club, Snug Harbor. I listened to the musicians to learn how to improve my skills. One night, they asked if anyone wanted to sit in on a set."

Darrian said yes and played with the group that night. At the end of the set, they asked if he could play again the next night. He said yes. After that gig, they invited him to play again. The next week, Darrian moved to New Orleans. He slept on a friend's couch so that he could continue to play gigs whenever possible.

Darrian's lucky break was the result of studying and practicing for years to develop his skills and then putting himself in places where he might have the opportunity to play. The evening at Snug Harbor which launched his career wasn't one lucky break. It was the culmination of years of preparation and intentional effort. He says, "What drives success is being in the right place at the right time and being prepared for the opportunity."

WHAT IS IT THEN?

Perhaps what determines success in achieving our goals is not as simple as we have been led to believe. Everyone has events in their lives that could be considered lucky or unlucky. Everyone has some form of talent. But only a small percentage achieve exceptional results. What is the secret to their success? I noticed one consistent factor across all the stories I heard.

The difference between an exceptional life and an average life is not the traits we're born with or the events we experience, but how we choose to respond to them. As a simple example, think of a game of poker. A player can win the pot with a good hand or a bad hand. It is not the cards they are dealt that determine their success, but rather the strategy they use to play the hand.

Jack Canfield, an American author, speaker, and entrepreneur explains the power of choosing our response using this success formula:[12]

E + R = O (Events + Responses = Outcomes)

The outcome, the result we get, is impacted by two basic things: the event, or something that happens, and our response to that event. Canfield explains, "If you want to change the results you get in the future, you must change how you respond to events in your life...starting today."[13]

Let's look at the example from my move to Los Angeles, and how a different response to the same event would have completely changed the outcome.

---

12   Jack Canfield, "The Formula that Puts You in Control of Success," *Jack Canfield's Blog*, accessed February 4, 2021.

13   Canfield, "The Formula that Puts You in Control of Success."

Event:	The rejection I received after the thirty-sixth job interview. I was running out of money, couldn't afford furniture, and completed job applications while sitting on the floor of a temporary apartment.
Response:	I could have responded by thinking that I just wasn't meant to live in Los Angeles. I could have believed that the job market was too competitive. It would have been easy and safe to give up and go home. Instead, I chose to apply for more jobs.
Outcome:	Interview number thirty-seven resulted in a fabulous job with a marketing agency at double my previous salary. It was the job that launched my career and my business.

I found out much later, I only got the interview appointment because my resume was on top of the pile when the hiring manager arrived at the office on Monday morning. Many people might consider that a lucky break. But I wouldn't have gotten the job without being prepared for the interview or without the right experience. My resume wouldn't have been on top of the pile if I had given up and started driving back to Virginia.

You can't always choose the events in your life, but you can improve your chances of being in the right place at the right time. More importantly, your response to any situation is completely within your control. How we choose to act or react in each situation in our life is a powerful predictor of our results.

BEING EXCEPTIONAL

Carol Dweck, Stanford Professor and author, explains how she helps freshman students learn about their heroes by giving them an assignment to research the person they admire. She says, "Almost invariably, they think that hero just catapulted to success, because of this amazing inborn talent. But every single time, they find that the hero put in inordinate amounts of work, met with obstacles, and really powered through them."[14] In her book, *Mindset: The New Psychology of Success*, Dweck says, "We like to think of our champions and idols as superheroes who were born different from us. We don't like to think of them as relatively ordinary people who made themselves extraordinary."[15]

We don't really want to know that success is a choice and is usually achieved through a lot of hard work and sacrifice. This information is not widely publicized in the media. Quite honestly, it is boring. It is not very exciting to hear about the thousands of hours of training or repetitive practice required to be a top performer. The people who have achieved amazing success were able to accomplish it through commitment, a huge amount of effort, focused practice, and willingness to keep trying until they succeeded.

Even when those stories are available, we often choose to ignore them. If we admit to ourselves that success is the result of incredible effort, it means we are choosing not to be exceptional simply because it is hard. It is more comfortable to believe that the people who have the life we want are the exception. Colvin points out, "If the activities that lead to greatness were easy and fun, then everyone would do them and they would not distinguish the best from the rest."[16]

---

14 *Talks at Google*, "The Growth Mindset: Carol Dweck," July 16, 2015, video, 47:25.

15 Carol Dweck, *Mindset: The New Psychology of Success* (New York: Ballantine Books, 2016), chap. 4, Kindle.

16 Colvin, *Talent is Overrated*, chap. 5.

When we take a hard look at people who lead exceptional lives, there's some good news and some bad news.

The bad news is:
- There is no magic formula. It takes time and consistent effort.
- It requires focus and commitment to pursue your goal.

The good news is:
- Success is not dependent on talent, luck, or other things beyond your control.
- You have the ability to create the outcomes you want.
- You can apply the same strategies that the "exceptions" do.

Taking a closer look at the stories of people who lead exceptional lives, I found they share key similarities even while taking different paths. They started in different situations and with different resources available to them. In many cases, they began with significant disadvantages. Rather than seeing those disadvantages as barriers or reasons to give up, they pushed harder and found ways around the obstacles in front of them. Each took a different path to success and even defined it differently. For some the goal was wealth or fame, for others it was excellent performance, and some were focused on contribution and purpose.

Regardless of the path they took or how they defined success, they all seemed to share a special kind of courage. It is not the kind of courage that enables someone to run into a burning building or fight off enemies. Instead, it is the courage to trust themselves and pursue their dream, without regard for what they are told they *should* do.

When I changed my life by starting over at forty-five, people told me I was brave. I didn't agree with them. Now I understand they were referring to this kind of courage. I have discovered that it is composed of seven specific ways of approaching life that anyone can learn and apply. Chapters 5 - 11 cover each of them in detail, along with strategies for how you can implement them in your life.

> We each have the power to choose an exceptional life aligned with our goals and dreams.

Before we can jump to the strategies, it is important to understand why more people don't already use them. The short and oversimplified reason is that it requires battling our natural instincts and the expectations we have of ourselves. Each component of courage helps to win this battle one step at a time and sets you on the path to creating the life you want.

SUMMARY

- Talent alone does not result in success. Often the most successful people are not the most talented.
- Luck is also not the most critical factor for success. You create your own opportunities.
- People who achieve exceptional results aren't different—they just do things differently.
- There are seven specific strategies, which anyone can apply to lead an exceptional life.

CHAPTER 2

STOP EXCEEDING
EXPECTATIONS

———

Nothing like that had ever happened before. Everyone heard it and saw it. My voice cracked noticeably multiple times, and tears filled the corners of my eyes. I didn't dare let them flow. I kept turning the moment over in my head in the taxi back to the airport. For no reason at all, I had almost cried in the middle of my presentation to the executive committee. As a business professional with over fifteen years of experience leading teams and giving presentations, I was mortified. Our quarterly results weren't great, but they were certainly nothing to cry about, especially for someone "strong" like me.

I slowly replayed the day. It seemed like so many others that it was barely memorable. I had crawled out of bed in the dark at 4 a.m. to get to the airport on time. I sleepwalked through the motions of the morning: brushed my teeth, put on my suit, grabbed a cup of coffee and my computer, then jumped into a taxi. Five hours later, I got out of a different taxi in front of the corporate headquarters in England.

I walked into the building prepared for a day of meetings with the managers from around Europe. There was nothing remarkable about the day. It was filled with far too many PowerPoint slides and far too few actual discussions. The only reprieve from the conference room's white walls was the short walk to the coffee machine at the end of the hall. The machine reluctantly produced a lukewarm brown liquid not even suitable for drinking, but it allowed a few moments for friendly conversation.

It didn't occur to me what had happened that day until hours later, when I sleepily stepped out of yet another taxi in front of my apartment late that evening. In the eighteen hours I had been awake, I had spent less than one hour doing something I wanted to do. A full 95 percent of my very long day had been spent fulfilling the expectations of other people.

I realized that the tears which surfaced in the middle of my presentation had been building up for months. They had nothing to do with the meeting's topic or the long day. My emotions had simply chosen an inopportune time to demand that I slow down and notice that I deserved to have more than 5 percent of my life for myself.

I had fallen into the trap of continually meeting or "exceeding" the expectations of everyone around me—friends, family, boss, and colleagues. I was using all my energy and effort to fulfill other people's goals. At the end of the day, I had nothing left for myself. I had been doing this for so long that I no longer even knew what my goals were.

It is a trap that many people fall into sooner or later. Life gets busy and moves quickly. There are important things to do, boxes to check, and tasks to complete. Everyone needs something from us, and we want to succeed and be liked. So, we get busy doing all the things faster, better, and more efficiently. We get caught up in the momentum of accomplishing lots of really important stuff, without paying much attention to the reasons we do it or what makes it so important.

Think about your day or week. How many hours did you spend doing something that you wanted to do? How many items on your to-do list are actually for you? How many hours were spent accomplishing what someone else wanted? And how many of those items will even be important a week from now?

EXPECTATIONS SERVE A PURPOSE

Expectations help us to anticipate outcomes. By definition, expectations are focused on some future occurrence or result. According to Merriam-Webster, to "expect" something means to consider it (a) probable or certain, (b) reasonable, due or necessary, or (c) bound in duty or obligation.[17]

Expectations play a critical role in making us feel more secure by giving us the sense that we can predictably rely on specific results or outcomes. Our expectations of the world around us and normal daily activities reduce feelings of uncertainty. This helps us to make decisions and react to situations more

---

17   *Merriam-Webster*, s.v. "expect (v.)," accessed February 4, 2021.

quickly and effectively.[18] Our expectations help to reduce the amount of information we need to evaluate in normal situations and conserve mental energy for processing new or more uncertain information.

For example, when you wake up in the morning, you most likely expect to have electricity and running water. When you turn on the coffee machine, you expect it to make coffee, and you expect that your car will start and reliably get you to work. If you had to begin each day wondering if these things would function reliably, just getting out of the house would be stressful and require much more thought and energy.

We use expectations throughout our day to help us make decisions efficiently. Let's say, I stop for a cup of coffee on my way to work and see a line of six people. Based on previous experience, I predict that getting my coffee will take ten minutes. Using that information, I decide if I have time to wait in line. If I choose to wait, I have an assumption of how the employee will communicate, how much the coffee should cost, and how to pay. These expectations make the process simple and easy to complete without much thought.

By contrast, buying a cup of coffee in a foreign country is more stressful, because it is unpredictable. I don't know with any certainty how long it will take, what the process is, or even what to say when ordering. Even my assumptions about how the coffee should taste may be incorrect. The experience

---

18   Andreja Bubic et al., "Prediction, Cognition and the Brain." *Frontiers in Human Neuroscience*, 4 no. 25 (March 22, 2010).

requires much more thought and attention to successfully get what I want. This is one reason that chain restaurants and coffee shops do so well. Their customers know exactly what to expect, regardless of which location they visit. It is predictable, easy, and low stress.

Of course, we don't only have expectations about the coffee machine and the traffic on the way to work. We also have expectations of ourselves and other people, and other people have expectations of us. This is an important distinction between types of expectations that shouldn't be overlooked. I find our expectations can be divided into two categories, based on whether they relate to objects and events or people and behaviors.

Impersonal expectations focus on the functioning of the world around us and are based primarily on facts or experience. They are easily defined or calculable and include things like how long it takes to drive to work, the weather in a particular region, how a certain food will taste, and so on. We can be relatively sure about these things, based on previous experience or information available to us.

Personal expectations focus on the behaviors or capabilities of ourselves and others. They are also based on previous experiences and information but aren't as simple to anticipate. They involve individual behaviors and have more variables. For example, my boss expects me to be excited about a promotion, you expect your spouse to remember your birthday, and I expect that engineers are good at math. In each case, these predictions of capability or behavior could be wrong.

Expectations influence our behavior in a wide variety of ways. They can push us to succeed or cause us to limit our options. They can help us be better humans that contribute to our community, or they can cause misjudgments that significantly impact our decisions. They are so prevalent in our daily lives that they affect almost everything we do, either consciously or unconsciously. For example, you go to work because you expect to get paid. You order a pizza because you expect it will taste good and satisfy your hunger. But perhaps you also passed up an opportunity for a new job because you anticipated you would fail. Or you didn't speak up at the team meeting because you expected your colleagues would think your idea was stupid.

THE PROBLEM WITH EXPECTATIONS

Expectations serve the important purpose of helping us to manage daily life more easily by anticipating outcomes, but they can also influence the outcomes. The problem with expectations is that we often form them without much thought. We make decisions based on these predictions and assumptions every day, and rarely stop to question where they come from or what impact they have on our results. And it is not only our own expectations we need to consider but also the expectations of the people around us.

A variety of sources throughout our lives help to inform and create our expectations. We develop expectations based on our own experiences and information from the people in our lives. Family, teachers, friends, and colleagues all have an influence on what we anticipate in our daily activities. Even nonpersonal sources of information can create powerful expectations. I have never been to Thailand, but I expect a specific climate, culture, and cuisine based on stories and pictures that I have heard and seen. Media in all forms, including social media, advertising, films, books, and more, can define the experiences we expect to have.

Regardless of the source, we all have expectations. They save mental energy by helping us to feel more certain throughout our day. They are a type of heuristic, or mental shortcut, which help us make decisions efficiently, but don't always guarantee an optimal outcome.[19] Most of the time these shortcuts reduce stress while producing acceptable results. In our daily lives, they can be especially effective when we are under time constraints or lack sufficient information.

We also use them when a situation appears familiar, and we feel we don't need to gather additional information. However, there are times where the "certainty" we feel about a particular outcome is flawed. We make sub-optimal decisions, due to cognitive biases, or systematic errors in rational judgment.[20] Cognitive biases impact our decisions and behaviors across all areas of our lives, and they occur across cultures and demographics. If not recognized and addressed, the combined power of these biases can lead us to make irrational decisions or behave in ways we aren't even aware of. We get "default" results that we didn't intend or seek consciously.[21]

---

19 APA Dictionary of Psychology, s.v. "heuristic (n.)," accessed February 7, 2021.

20 Cambridge Dictionary, s.v. "cognitive bias (n.)," accessed February 28, 2021.

21 Chris Berdick, Mind Over Mind: The Surprising Power of Expectations (New York: Penguin, 2012), Kindle.

PROBLEM 1: WE GET WHAT WE EXPECT

The concept of a self-fulfilling prophecy is probably familiar to you. It occurs when an existing inaccurate belief or expectation causes its own fulfillment.[22]

One common example is the placebo effect. When patients receive an inactive pill which they believe is medicine, they often report feeling better, even without any real medication. They expect the "medicine" to work and then experience that result. The phenomenon of the placebo effect was first studied in 1784 by a commission led by Benjamin Franklin in Paris.[23] Centuries later, it still impacts patient results today and continues to be studied.

Of course, we also experience self-fulfilling prophecies in our daily lives. Our expectations have more power to influence our results than we usually consider. For example, if I believe that I will do badly in an interview, my own nervousness and doubts will result in presenting myself poorly to the interviewer. Our expectations of others are also powerful. What begins as an inaccurate assumption can result in behavior aligned with that assumption. People often live up or down to our expectations of them.

PROBLEM 2: WE SEEK CONFIRMATION

We have a natural tendency to seek out and focus on information that is consistent with our existing beliefs, known as confirmation bias.[24]

---

22 *Encyclopedia Britannica*, s.v. "Self-fulfilling prophecy," August 1, 2016.
23 Berdick, *Mind Over Mind*, prelude.
24 *Encyclopedia Britannica*, s.v. "Confirmation bias," October 9, 2019.

It is often noticed in the context of research. The researcher unconsciously treats the participants differently, resulting in behavior aligned with the researcher's prediction. In one example, university students were given rats and told that they needed to train them to complete a maze. They were given two groups of rats and told that one group was the "smart" group and the other group was the "dull" group, even though there was no difference. At the end of the experiment, the "smart" rats were actually more successful because they had been trained differently than the "dull" rats.[25]

Notice that this bias not only affected the results for the researcher but also influenced the behavior and results of the "participants." The impact of confirmation bias has also been studied related to how stereotypes of students affect their performance in school.

Confirmation bias is prevalent in all areas of our lives. It causes us to interpret information to support our beliefs, especially when the topic is important to us.[26] For example, if I believe that crime in my city is increasing, I am more likely to pay attention to news about robberies. I may dismiss or ignore positive stories about the community and focus only on the negative. On my way to work, I might interpret someone innocently approaching me to ask for directions as a threat.

---

25 R. Rosenthal & K. L. Fode, "The Effect of Experimenter Bias on the Performance of the Albino Rat," *Behavioral Science, 8*(3), (1963):183–189.

26 *Encyclopedia Britannica*, s.v. "Confirmation bias," October 9, 2019.

PROBLEM 3: WE OVERLOOK IMPORTANT INFORMATION

Expectation bias, along with confirmation bias, can cause incorrect beliefs to persist, even when information is available to the contrary.[27] This is especially true in situations where a person is completing a task which is routine for them. Our daily experiences reinforce our beliefs and can give us a false sense of certainty about routine situations. When we repeat a task often, we expect the information to be the same each time and can miss other critical information. The result is that we feel certain about decisions we've made based on incorrect perceptions of the situation.

An analysis of pilot deviations revealed several incidents where pilot errors were determined to be the result of expectation bias. For example, in January 2014 a plane landed at the wrong airport in Branson, Missouri. "The flight crew expected that the visually identified airport and runway were the intended destination and did not reference cockpit displays to verify the airport and runway."[28] Even though the correct information was available, they overlooked it. The good news is that by being aware of this expectancy bias, training can be developed specifically to help overcome it through active questioning.[29]

There are tactics that can help catch and correct these biases by actively engaging our focus on the details of the situation. One way to do this is by saying the information out loud. Instead of only thinking it, you are now

---

27 "Flight Crew Expectation Bias," Skybrary, last modified September 4, 2019 at 9:10.

28 Ibid.

29 Ibid.

speaking and hearing the details, engaging more senses. You can also actively question information by using "why" or "how" questions.

EXPECTATIONS AS OBLIGATIONS

It is not only our own expectations that influence results but also the assumptions others have about what we *should* do. The expectations others have of us influence us differently, depending on how we perceive them. If we believe they are true or realistic, we act accordingly. However, when the expectations are not aligned with our values or perceptions, they create an internal conflict between what we believe and how we feel pressured to behave. We are torn between our own desires and what we are being told. In this case, these expectations shift from being "probable or reasonable" to the third definition provided by Merriam-Webster, and we become "bound in duty or obligation."[30]

Many expectations related to our capabilities and behaviors are not ours. They are given to us, or thrust upon us, by the people in our lives or the media we consume. They are the goals, opinions, and beliefs of other people, and we consciously or unconsciously accept and internalize them as our own. These expectations are often not aligned with our values and cause a great deal of stress. We are stuck trying to balance our desire to fulfill what is expected against what we want for ourselves.

---

30 *Merriam-Webster*, s.v. "expect (v.)," accessed February 4, 2021.

Machiko is a successful young Japanese woman who achieved her goal of living and working in New York City, but only after years of battling the expectations of her family and culture. In our conversation, she described the moment she finally had the freedom to pursue her dream. She recalls, "I felt as if a huge weight I'd been carrying for years was finally lifted, and I could breathe again."

Machiko grew up in a rural town north of Tokyo with strong culture and traditions. She explained that when she finished school, the next steps were already clearly defined: get married, have children, and live close to family. She told me, "If you are thirty and single, something is wrong with you." The pressure didn't only come from her parents, but also her friends, who were already married and starting families. They couldn't understand why she wasn't also following this traditional path.

But that wasn't what she wanted. After completing her studies in New York, she was certain she wanted to live there. Marrying a man in the small community where her family lived would permanently block that possibility. She tried to reduce the obligation she felt to her parents by paying for her own studies and expenses, but the burden of responsibility was still present. For years, she searched for a solution, but the pressure to marry and settle down in Japan increased. The small ways she found to push back wouldn't be sustainable. I asked her what had finally changed that made her move to New York possible. She told me that her mother had been diagnosed with breast cancer. Machiko recalled, "Shortly after she began treatments, she said to me one day, 'Machiko, you should do what makes you happy, not what is expected of you.'"

After a year of treatment, Machiko's mother is well again. Machiko succeeded in creating the life she wanted to live, with both a career in New York and her family's approval. Her persistent focus on her goals, despite her family's expectations, was rewarded.

PERSUASION VS. ATTRIBUTION

Research has found that subtle differences in our perception of an expectation impact our behavior and results. In several studies done with students, this subtle difference consistently influenced behavior. In one study, a group of fifth graders was encouraged not to litter and to clean up their surroundings. A teacher repeatedly told half of the group that they were neat and tidy people. The other half of the group was told that they should be neat and tidy.[31]

The statements made to the first group, described as attribution, express a character trait in the present tense as a fact. These statements were significantly more effective in changing behavior than the statements made to the second group.[32] Those statements, described as persuasion, use the word *should*. This implies that they are not yet neat and tidy. Rather, it is something they ought to be at some point in the future.

As part of the same research, another study focused specifically on school performance and self-esteem. A class

---

31 R.L. Miller, P. Brickman, and D. Bolen, "Attribution versus Persuasion as a Means for Modifying Behavior," *J Pers Soc Psychol*. 31, no. 3 (March 1975): 430-41.

32 Ibid.

of second graders was split into three groups, and each group was repeatedly encouraged with different types of statements.[33]

Group 1 heard things like, "You **are** really good in math." (attribution)

Group 2 was told things like, "You **should be** really good in math." (persuasion)

Group 3 heard statements like, "Excellent work! I am really happy about your progress." (neutral)

The students who performed the best were the students in Group 1.[34] These statements were more effective because they created an assumption that the students accepted as true. They believed that they "are good." The statements for Group 2 were concluded to be less effective because changing one word from "are" to "should" created a gap between the current state and the desired state (a person should be what he is not).

The question is, whose assumptions do you accept as true? Are their expectations in line with your aspirations for yourself and your true capabilities? Or have you fallen into the trap of internalizing the beliefs and assumptions of everyone around you?

---

33   Ibid.
34   Ibid.

STOP EXCEEDING EXPECTATIONS. OVERCOME THEM.
Expectations in both our personal and business lives have increased dramatically in the past several decades. Customer service is supposed to be faster and friendlier, products are supposed to be better and cheaper, and you are supposed to get more work done in less time. It is everywhere around us. We are constantly reminded that we need to give 110 percent. The minute we achieve a goal, someone moves the bar higher.

These ever-growing expectations put us in a position of needing to accomplish more and more with the same amount of time, energy, and mental capacity. In the corporate world, it is no longer enough to meet expectations. Now we are told to go above and beyond in order to exceed them. There is no space to celebrate an achievement. After all, everyone expected you to do that, so there is nothing remarkable about it. The pressure to achieve higher and higher targets can be overwhelming, and it feels as if we are never doing enough.

In her book *Stressed Out Girls*, psychologist Roni Cohen-Sandler found that this desire to constantly exceed expectations was especially a problem for teenage girls. She points out that "[they] are prone to becoming estranged from their inner lives. What I mean is that even teens who are driven to achieve are so busy living up to others' expectations that they either don't develop or eventually relinquish their own goals[...] They barely know who they are or who they want to become."[35]

---

35 Roni Cohen-Sandler, *Stressed Out Girls: Helping Them Thrive in the Age of Pressure* (New York: Viking / Penguin Group, 2006), 25.

Shelley, a coach who helps students prepare their college applications, says that she also notices this tension. She explained, "Even the kids who have managed to develop a clear sense of themselves and what they want often feel pressured about what they *should* do by parents or other people in their lives." For example, parents will pressure their kids to go to a certain school, even when the school's specialty or culture is not a fit for the student's goals or personality.

After years of working with students, Shelley made an interesting observation. She noticed that often this pressure from parents has nothing to do with having high goals for their child. Instead, the parents themselves are feeling concerned about their own image in the community and how their success as parents is perceived by others. They are projecting their own *shoulds* onto their children. What happens? The student goes to a school that is a bad match for them because it "looks good." Then they struggle in their studies, or in their social life, or both. It has exactly the opposite of the intended effect—resulting in a less confident and less successful young adult.

From my observations and experience, we are running ourselves into the ground to meet everyone's expectations but our own. Or worse, we are busily exceeding expectations that were simply wrong or misinformed from the start.

Instead of exceeding expectations we need to overcome them. When we slow down long enough to question the beliefs, assumptions, and demands placed on us, we can begin to recognize the biases and fallacies they bring with them. We can begin to see the limitations and burden that they place upon us.

We have the power to disagree with the opinion others have of us and set our own expectations. We can also shift our perspective to better understand the source. Often, the expectations of the people around us reflect their goals and agenda, which may or may not be aligned with what we want for ourselves.

You can spend your whole life working hard to meet someone else's expectations or choose to spend your time and energy pursuing your aspirations. Take time to notice the difference. Only then can you begin to choose which expectations to exceed and which to overcome.

Expectations show up in our lives as a collection of *shoulds*, which promise a happy life if we just follow their directives. In the next chapters, we'll uncover the various ways these *shoulds* emerge and why they are so difficult to banish.

SUMMARY

- Expectations serve an important purpose and make routine decisions easier.
- Cognitive biases cause us to distort information to align with our expectations.
- Expectations affect our behavior and the behavior of others, impacting results.
- Misalignment of expectations and our values creates stress and obligation.
- Awareness creates space to choose which expectations to exceed and which to overcome.

CHAPTER 3

THE SEVEN DEADLY SHOULDS

——

Have you ever wondered why 80 percent of people who make New Year's resolutions have given up on them before we've even reached February?[36] Or why fitness is a $100 billion global industry, but almost 40 percent of adults are overweight, and obesity has tripled since 1975.[37][38]

If we know what we *should* do to be happier, healthier, and more successful, why don't we do it? Why do our good intentions and willpower fail us so often?

I believe that most people fail at these goals because of *should*. Should represents the gap between some future ideal and the current situation, bridged by obligation. It is the difference

---

36   Kelsey Mulvey, "80% of New Year's Resolutions Fail by February - Here's How to Keep Yours," *Business Insider,* January 4, 2017.

37   Christina Gough, "Health and Fitness Clubs Statistics & Facts," Statista, Nov. 16, 2020.

38   World Health Organization, "Obesity and Overweight," April 1, 2020.

between your current behavior and the behavior you want or someone wants for you.

Unlike expectations, which imply a probable or certain result, should implies that something is not currently ideal and needs to be changed. The hidden promise of should is that if I do this certain thing, I will get the desired result, and everything will work out well.

Notice two things about this. First, every time we *should* do something, it reinforces that the present condition is somehow lacking. The word immediately brings with it a dissatisfaction. Second, it already dictates a specific result, leaving no room for exploration or alternate possibilities. It often focuses on a specific manifestation of the goal rather than the underlying motivations for the goal.

Let's take a closer look at a common example: "I should lose weight."

Every time I say this to myself or hear it from someone else, it is a reminder that something is wrong with me. It might be true that my health would improve if I lost weight. However, *should* simultaneously emphasizes I have failed and puts my desired result at some unclear point in the future.

The statement also jumps to a specific outcome, rather than exploring options to achieve the underlying goal. Losing weight is only a tactic to achieve some other goal, such as being healthier, looking better in my clothes, or being more attractive to a potential partner. If my true goal is to be healthier, and I lose weight by going on a crash diet, I have accomplished the opposite of my intention. Other ways of becoming healthier, better aligned with my values, have been excluded or ignored.

In 1950, German psychoanalyst Karen Horney coined the phrase "the tyranny of the shoulds."[39] She described shoulds as inner dictates that are the dividers between our ideal self and our real self. According to Horney, when we sense that we are not fulfilling these self-imposed requirements of our ideal self, our inner critic surfaces to remind us that we *should* be better.

Almost a century later, these inner critics are still causing as much chaos as they did when she first wrote about them. We spend our whole lives developing our specific *shoulds*. They are first planted in our awareness by parents, teachers, and others in our community with the noble purpose of helping us to be proper humans.

They remind us to do things that keep us healthy, kind, and safe:
- You should eat your vegetables.
- You should share your toys.
- You should not play with fire.

As we get older and gather various life experiences, we collect new *shoulds* along the way. These are generally meant to help us transition more smoothly into adulthood:
- You should only spend what you can afford.

---

39 Karen Horney, *Neurosis and Human Growth: The Struggle Toward Self-Realization* (New York: W. W. Norton & Company, Inc., 1991 edition).

- You should get a good job.
- You should wear pants to work.

By the time we reach our twenties or thirties, we have a whole collection of *shoulds* dancing around in our heads, influencing our daily activities and decisions. Sometimes they are relatively calm and quiet, but often they jump with limitless energy between our conscious and subconscious thoughts and influence almost everything we do. Some people have only a few *shoulds*, while other people struggle with a whole team of them.

They often originate from something someone said or an experience we've had, but we express them as our own beliefs. They are all working to keep us safe in some way, either by pushing us to achieve more, helping us fit in, or ensuring that we avoid risk. Eventually, we experience them so frequently, from so many different sources, that we barely notice them.

The strategies of your *shoulds* are designed to help you survive, but they will not help you to thrive. To properly tame them, you first need to recognize them.

THE PYRAMID OF *SHOULDS*

While organizing my interview notes, I saw something that surprised me. I noticed that the things we feel most compelled or obligated to do roughly align with Maslow's Hierarchy of Needs. Abraham Maslow introduced the concept in 1943 in his paper, "A Theory of Human Motivation." The theory proposes that there are five categories of needs that motivate all human behavior.[40]

Although there are some criticisms of the concept, it has become widely known and used in business and education. Maslow's theory represented a significant shift in psychology from a focus on what caused people to be unwell toward research on what motivates healthy behaviors and contributes to overall wellness and satisfaction.[41]

It makes sense that the things we feel most compelled to do would satisfy fundamental human needs and that these needs would motivate our behaviors. These behaviors are intended to bring us closer to our ideal situation, which would mean having all levels of our needs fulfilled.

I found that most of our *shoulds* fulfill one or more of the categories of needs which Maslow proposed, ranging from basic physiological needs (food, water, shelter) to more abstract self-actualization needs (purpose), generally depicted in a pyramid.[42]

---

40   Abraham H. Maslow, "A Theory of Human Motivation," *Psychological Review, 50*(4), (1943): 370–396.
41   Kendra Cherry, "The 5 Levels of Maslow's Hierarchy of Needs," *Verywell Mind,* June 3, 2020.
42   Maslow, "A Theory of Human Motivation," 370–396.

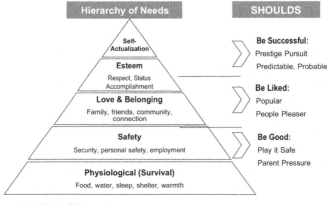

Maslow's Hierarchy of Needs

BE GOOD. (SAFETY AND SURVIVAL SHOULDS)

Aligned with the basic needs at bottom of the pyramid are the *shoulds* which tell us to be good and follow the rules. These behaviors keep us safe from danger and ensure that our basic survival needs are met. We experience these first as small children, and they become strong quickly because they come from a place of actual authority. When we begin to question what we are told, it often results in a negative response or even punishment. These are intended to ensure that we don't jeopardize our basic needs for food and shelter, and we survive long enough to experience the higher levels of the pyramid.

Parent Pressure:	Our parents or family are likely the single biggest influence in our lives. They are the first people we trust, and they are the ones that teach us about what to expect from life. They teach us that fire is hot, cookies are for after dinner, and rules are made to be followed. They protect us from danger and generally want the best for us. Their desire for us to have a good life is expressed in a lot of *shoulds*, usually with a good dose of obligation. You should go to college, you should study medicine, and you should get married and start a family.
Play It Safe:	These *shoulds* draw their strength from all the experts in your life: teachers, bosses, and other authorities. They will tell you the "right" way to do things based on their expertise. They are especially active when you are under pressure, and there's a whole army of them. "They" seem to know everything, but no one is sure how they know. For what it is worth, "they" also said the world was flat, cigarettes weren't addictive, and pineapple on pizza was a good idea.

These *shoulds* are clever. When they tap you on the shoulder to say you *should* do something, they appear to be helpful and concerned for your well-being. Regardless of the source, they have a vested and somewhat selfish interest in you following the rules. After all, if you behave badly or fail at an important task, it looks as though they aren't doing their job well.

BE LIKED. (LOVE AND BELONGING SHOULDS)

Since many people already have basic safety and security needs fulfilled, the *shoulds* related to acceptance, love, and belonging are especially powerful. They are focused on fitting in and being accepted among the social groups important to us. They draw their cues from the world around us, including family traditions, cultural norms, and pressure from peers. They can be positive or negative and show up everywhere—at work, with friends, and in our family and romantic relationships. If we try to ignore them, they threaten us with loneliness, bullying, or fear of missing out.

They use two basic strategies to satisfy their unquenchable quest to be liked.

People-pleaser: These *shoulds* ensure that no one has a reason to dislike you. They remind you not to rock the boat or express an opinion that might be unpopular. Their favorite word is "yes," and they are the first to chime in when a colleague asks you to work late or a friend asks for help moving. Their motto is, "If you can't agree, don't say anything at all." They'll remind you that you should make a point to tell your boss how great his idea is, even if it doubles your workload.

Popular: These *shoulds* take a more proactive approach—be liked by fitting in. They can be found hanging out with the "cool kids" most of the time and love attention. They'll be at your side at the mall, telling you that you should buy the latest iPhone or that you need the trendiest fashion. They'll remind you that you should live in the "right" neighborhood, and you should make sure to be seen at the currently popular cafe, bar, or vegan restaurant.

They seem friendly and helpful, but they are secretly sabotaging you. If you are always saying yes to what everyone else wants, you never prioritize what is important to you. You work hard to do all the things you should do and have no energy left for your own goals. Worse, you've forgotten what you really think because you've been too busy agreeing with everyone else.

BE SUCCESSFUL. (ESTEEM SHOULDS)

Motivation to be successful is generally perceived as positive. However, the concept of success is relative and is influenced by the people and messages around us. These messages can be overt or subtle and are based in cultural and societal definitions of success related to intelligence, physical ability, money, power, influence, and other factors.

These influences evolve into a variety of *shoulds*, which attempt to ensure our success, and they show up in three primary ways:

Predictable: These shoulds have it easy. They just follow the path everyone else has taken and tell you to do the same. They don't like to take risks and prefer to know exactly what to expect. They are also a bit lazy and prefer not to think too hard. They like wide, well-paved roads with clear directions so that the journey is smooth. They are also quick to point out what you should not do. Their mantra is "follow the directions." You might not discover anything new, but at least you will be safe and won't get lost.

Probable: Also afraid of uncertainty, they like to take the safe bet. They jump in when there is no proven path to follow, and some decision has to be made. These shoulds claim to have a foolproof way of calculating the odds and knowing which direction is best. They'll tell you that you shouldn't start a business because 50 percent of new businesses fail in the first year (they are wrong). Or will remind you that you shouldn't trust a partner because the last one betrayed you. They rely on the available data to bet on your best chances of success.

Prestige Pursuit: Being more of the jealous type, these shoulds are never satisfied and always want more. They will whisper in your ear that you should have the fancy house, the fast car, or the corner office. As soon as you reward them with one trophy, they start asking for the next one. They are disappointed with the wonderful things you already have because someone else has something better.

Most people have a few dominant *shoulds*, and some people carry around a whole team of them. The collection of esteem *shoulds* we carry around with us creates an immense amount of pressure to be more, do more, and achieve more, often in direct conflict with our values. Our inner critic will pop up regularly to remind us that we are falling behind, other people are doing it better, and we are not good enough.

* * *

GOALS AND MOTIVATIONS

Now back to those New Year's resolutions that so many people set but fail to achieve. Many people will propose that you don't achieve these goals because your willpower wasn't strong enough, and you weren't committed to your goal. I am going to suggest that it is not your willpower that is failing you, it is your motivation to fulfill one specific need over another.

For example, I set a resolution to go to the gym after work. My motivation for this goal is to be healthier and feel better (physiological). On my way out of the office, friends invite me to join them for dinner and drinks. I decide to skip the gym and go out with my friends in direct contrast to my goal. Being able to immediately satisfy my need for love and belonging has overruled my need to be healthier in the future.

Often the need satisfied by our current behavior is more relevant and immediate than the need that would be fulfilled by the new behavior. We are motivated by the stronger need.

Face it, if you really wanted to do it, you wouldn't have to bribe or compel yourself with a resolution. You would simply start doing it. It is a reasonably safe bet that there aren't many New Year's resolutions to eat more cake, drink more wine, and exercise less.

Could it be that you are not achieving your goals because they are not actually *your* goals? Are they something that you think you *should* do rather than something you actually want to do?

Harvard Psychologist, Susan David, describes this as the difference between "have to" goals and "want to" goals. "Have to" goals are something we feel obliged to do, generally because somebody told us we should do it.[43] Think of the last time you resolved to lose weight, eat healthier, or get more exercise. You felt obligated to do these things, most likely because your doctor or spouse told you to. Or you felt pressure from friends or all those pictures of perfect beach bodies on social media. In any case, these goals are externally motivated—someone else has set them for you—even if you have reluctantly taken ownership of them.

The problem with "have to" goals is that they often get overruled by our brain because we don't have enough importance attached to the results. It is not that we are weak, but our willpower doesn't get a chance. Our brain has made the decision before our willpower is even engaged.[44]

In contrast, "want to" goals are aligned with our values and our purpose.[45] These goals are internally motivated because

---

43 *RSA*, "RSA Replay: Emotional Agility," streamed live on April 7, 2016, video, 58:24.

44 Ibid.

45 Ibid.

they help us achieve something that has significant meaning for us. Even if it is the same goal, the motivation and our internal perception of the goal is different, and we are much more likely to succeed.

A while ago, I met my friend Kate for lunch and saw an example of this difference firsthand. I had worked and traveled with Kate for years, and the majority of our conversations took place standing in the courtyard or sitting on a balcony. Why? Kate smoked a lot. Despite the health risks, this habit actually held a lot of personal benefits for her. She constantly met colleagues from other teams while standing outside to smoke. When we went out, she always met new people easily, simply by asking someone for a light. She was making new friends outside, while I was standing inside watching her purse.

Kate talked about giving up smoking for years. Once, she even made a bet with some colleagues to stop smoking for six weeks. I think it lasted two days. For all the talk about being healthier and saving money on cigarettes, Kate didn't really want to give up smoking, but she felt like she should.

When she and I next met for lunch, it had been months since I'd seen her in person. I picked a table outside, even though the weather was cold and windy. I knew that she would want to smoke. As she arrived, she asked, "Why are you sitting outside?" I explained my reasons for choosing the table, and she replied, "Oh, that's not necessary, I stopped smoking months ago!"

We moved to a warmer table inside the café, and I asked what had changed her mind about smoking. To my surprise, she had learned a few months earlier that she was now pregnant with her first child. She stopped smoking immediately and hadn't had another cigarette. From that moment, it wasn't something she *should* do; it was something she wanted to do. It was no longer about her own health or the money it could save. It was about the health of her child. Her goal and motivation had changed from a have-to goal (what other people believed she should do) to a want-to goal (what was important to her). Willpower was no longer required.

The key to achieving our goals is to first make sure that they are *our* goals and not *shoulds* that we have acquired along the way.

The *shoulds* that we adopt as children and carry into adulthood grow stronger because we feed them and nurture them in an attempt to gain security, love, and esteem. But we are getting the opposite result. We allow them to drive us toward ever-increasing levels of insecurity, isolation, and uncertainty.

Recognizing the sources of our *shoulds* and the havoc they cause in our lives is the first step to banishing them and replacing them with more powerful words and thoughts. We can eliminate the inner critic which is constantly poking us with thoughts of obligation and regret and begin to embrace being ourselves. Once the pattern is evident, we can actively choose motivations aligned with our values and drive behaviors that achieve our goals. We have the chance to have a life filled with confidence, connection, and courage once we move beyond *should*. The next chapters will give you specific strategies to tame the *shoulds* and confidently pursue your goals.

SUMMARY

- Should is the gap between your current situation and some ideal situation.
- We acquire *shoulds* from multiple sources, including experiences, other people, and media.
- *Shoulds* are intended to help us fulfill our basic human needs, but they are flawed.
- Goals are easier to achieve when they are aligned with your values, rather than your *shoulds*.
- Once you recognize *shoulds,* you can replace them with more powerful motivators.

CHAPTER 4

TAMING THE SHOULDS

We've gotten so caught up in hacking our lives that we've lost sight of why we're doing it. As a population, we've become more overwhelmed, unhealthy, and unhappy than ever before.[46]

We are putting more and more pressure on ourselves to be what the world tells us we should be, and it is making us miserable. This syndrome has been infecting our lives since approximately the time technology enabled us to become more efficient, more informed, and better able to compare ourselves to everyone else on the planet. Ironically, the advancements enabling us to be safer, more connected, and more successful have instead increased the gap between the life we have and the life we believe we *should* have.

Shoulds serve a purpose in our lives. They do things like motivate us to go jogging when we would rather watch Netflix or kitten videos. They remind us to be upstanding members

---

46 John F. Helliwell, Richard Layard and Jeffrey D. Sachs, *World Happiness Report 2019* (New York: Sustainable Development Solutions Network, 2019), chap. 5.

of the community and to contribute something of value. They also do their best to keep us safe from embarrassment, rejection, bankruptcy, and hot stoves, among other things. They are meant to help us get our needs fulfilled, but they are doing a terrible job of it.

Young adults who are striving to do everything they *should* to succeed in school are so stressed-out and exhausted that they develop eating disorders, depression, and even suicidal thoughts. In fact, a study conducted for the past three decades reports that the overall sense of health and well-being by incoming college freshmen has been declining steadily for the past fifteen years. Women are more affected than men and are feeling more overwhelmed than ever. In 2017, more than half of incoming female students (51 percent) reported frequently feeling overwhelmed by all they had to do in the previous year (compared to 22.6 percent in 1985).[47]

In our efforts to be what we think we *should* be, we've lost ourselves and our ability to create meaningful connections. In her now famous TEDx Talk on vulnerability, Brené Brown discusses her research on human connection, love, and belonging.[48] She discovered that people who have a strong sense of love and belonging do a few things differently. Among them was, "they had connection, and—this was the hard part—as a result of authenticity, they were

---

47 "The Mental and Physical Well-Being of Incoming Freshmen: Three Decades of Research," *Higher Education Today,* September 6, 2018.

48 Brené Brown, "The Power of Vulnerability," filmed June 2010 in Houston, TX, TED video, 20:04.

willing to let go of who they thought they should be in order to be who they were."[49]

THE PROBLEM WITH SHOULDS

Despite trying to ensure we are safe and successful, *shoulds* are also troublemakers and can contribute a significant amount of stress and unhappiness to our lives. When we give them our attention, they create a lot of pressure to be, do, or obtain something other than what we currently have. We beat ourselves up (I should be stronger), blame ourselves for something that didn't go well (I should have worked harder), or create limitations (I should be satisfied with this job). Projecting *shoulds* onto other people or events (he should have remembered my birthday) creates dissatisfaction with a situation over which we have little control.

THEY FOCUS ON THE FUTURE OR THE PAST, RATHER THAN THE PRESENT

Should is not an action. It is the favorite word of your inner critic, but there is nothing you can do to resolve it. The word is always focused on something that already happened (I should have asked for more money) or something that ought to happen in the future (I should go jogging). It creates an endless source of stress, reminding you that there is some goal not achieved or something that could have gone better.

It is a thought that dances through our consciousness to remind us that we have not reached a goal, but it creates

---

49 *Ibid.*

no action. It is the difference between doing something and thinking about doing something. Waking up each morning thinking, "I should go to work" doesn't accomplish anything. Your current situation is only affected when you take a clear action and go to work.

THEY ARE RISK-AVERSE AND CAUSE COMPLACENCY

If we do what we should do and get undesirable results, we have a built-in excuse for failure. When we follow the rules and take the proven path, then failure cannot be our fault. Following our *shoulds* gives us the comfort and excuse that we are doing all the "right" things based on some outside influence or authority. There is very little personal ownership of our actions. We do what someone else told us we should or follow the cultural norms and expectations. We can very comfortably shift the blame to someone else. Even as adults, the child in us wants the security of being able to say, "But he told me to do it" or "Everyone else was doing it."

Shoulds are also highly concerned with the odds of success. They claim to have a foolproof way to calculate the risk and predict the safest path to the goal. But the information they use is incomplete and based on a limited number of experiences. So, while their evaluation of risk appears very scientific, the truth is exactly the opposite. The world is changing quickly. Making decisions today based on what happened when we were younger, or worse, what other people told us happened to them, relies on outdated and inaccurate information. It is like trying to drive from New York to California using a map from the 1980s. Some of the main roads are there, but a significant amount of critical information would be missing.

THEY STOP US FROM THINKING FOR OURSELVES

We become so conditioned to blindly or begrudgingly follow the advice of our *shoulds* that we are too busy to question why we're following their guidance. We often play along because it is easy and requires less energy to do what we are told we should do, rather than define our own solution. We simply have to follow directions and check the boxes. We don't need to think about a situation, weigh the various options, and make an informed choice. In doing so, we don't see alternative options available to us.

Pause for a moment and think about it. How much of your day today was spent making conscious, thoughtful decisions about your actions? And how much of your time was spent crossing the things you should do off your to-do list? How many of those activities were based on obligations or other people's needs and expectations of you?

* * *

CURING THE *SHOULD* SYNDROME

The good news is that we can tame our *shoulds* by changing the strategies we use to fulfill our needs for safety, security, belonging, and success.

A friend described it this way: "Going through life with our *shoulds* is like taking a road trip with a bunch of children. They all want something different, and they want it now." She explained how they hijack our journey, steering us in directions and detours that aren't our intended destination. They each have an opinion that is worth listening to and acknowledging, but you can't let them drive the car. She told me, "You have to put the kids in the back seat and promise that everyone will get their favorite flavor of ice cream. Then you can take the wheel and drive confidently toward your destination without their constant interruptions."

The people I interviewed had all found ways to successfully overcome the typical traps of *should*. Even though they came from a wide variety of situations and cultures, they shared similar strategies. In Part 2, you will discover how they used these strategies to change careers, launch successful businesses, move to other countries, or pursue a passion. They didn't follow fast formulas for success but rather approached their goals with persistence and a focus on their destination.

You'll see how they also met the basic needs of safety, security, belonging, and esteem, but from a different perspective than *should*. The strategies they used spring from the natural tendencies we have as young children to be confident, curious, and bold. They work because their power comes from within rather than from outside sources. We only need time to uncover and embrace them.

In order to thrive instead of simply survive, these people used COURAGE to create exceptional lives. COURAGE is an acronym for the strategies I found they shared. Part 2 explores these strategies and how you can immediately apply them to create the life you want.

The next chapters can be read in any order, as they each focus on one particular strategy to move beyond *should*.

You can jump ahead to the ones that speak most to your situation or read along in order to learn how ordinary people created exceptional lives by taking a different approach than most.

SHOULDS		BEYOND SHOULD
• Prestige Pursuit • Predictable / Probable	BE SUCCESSFUL Self-Actualization & Accomplishment	Clarity of Purpose: *Redefine Success (Ch 5)* Overcome Expectations: *Rethink Possible (Ch 6)*
• Popular • People Pleaser	BE LIKED Love & Belonging	Unapologetically Authentic: *Reject Normal (Ch 7)* Return on Risk: *Reconsider Risk (Ch 8)*
• Play it Safe • Parent Pressure	BE GOOD Safety, Security, Survival	Accelarate Action: *Regain Momentum (Ch 9)* Grow through Challenge: *Reimagine Failure (Ch 10)* Embrace being yourself: *Reinvent your Life (Ch 11)*

EXCEPTIONAL: Thrive rather than survive

PART 2

THE STORY WE COULD CREATE

Clarity of Purpose
Redefine Success

Overcome Expectations
Rethink Possible

Unapologetically Authentic
Reject Normal

Return on Risk
Reconsider Risk

Accelerate Action
Regain Momentum

Grow through Challenge
Reimagine Failure

Embrace being Yourself
Reinvent Your Life

Clarity of Purpose

Overcome Expectations

Unapologetically Authentic

Return on Risk

Accelerate Action

Grow through Challenge

Embrace being Yourself

CHAPTER 5

REDEFINE SUCCESS

---

*"Don't be afraid to give up the
good to go for the great."*

- JOHN D. ROCKEFELLER

What if holding on to who you think you *should* be is keeping you from becoming the person you want to be?

I have some good news. You are already exceptional. You have a combination of experiences, skills, talents, and genetics that no one else on the planet has. You bring a unique perspective to the world. Just as there is no average fingerprint, there is also no average person.

Before you start disagreeing with me, let me be clear—there are plenty of people who get average results, earn average salaries, and lead average lives. And by most common measures of success, I would be considered one of them. I have not made millions on the IPO of a start-up, I am not a movie star or an influencer, and I haven't won a gold medal or developed a new technology. What I have done is followed an unconventional path to achieving my goals—a path which many people consider exceptional.

I would argue that success is not defined by wealth, awards, and fame but is instead by fulfillment, connection, and contribution. I have chosen to create my own definition of success, and it has led me on a journey that many people have told me they envy and even consider brave. Once per decade, I have completely reinvented my life and career. I have founded and run a successful business, lived in multiple countries, and had the privilege of making friends all over the world. One's definition of success is subjective and personal. You can choose your own or accept the definitions provided by family, friends, and media.

The people who we think of as exceptional have embraced being the exception. They don't settle for the same results that everyone else gets, and they don't take the same path. They focus on what is possible instead of probable and set out to achieve it with no excuses. They are often seen as rebellious, selfish, or wildly optimistic. Regardless of how you label it, they rarely accept the "realistic" view about what it is possible to achieve. For that reason, they achieve exceptional things.

Many people get stuck at "good enough." They have a good job and a good life. Sometimes they even have a fabulous career and a life that looks perfect to everyone else. They are told repeatedly they should be satisfied with that. Of course, many people are satisfied with conventional success, and there is absolutely nothing wrong with that. An unconventional path is not right for everyone. I am only suggesting that you consider if it is the life you chose or the one you are settling for. The life that is good enough for other people may not be the life that makes you feel happy and fulfilled.

Victor was one of those people who had achieved the common definition of success. Despite starting his career with several biases against him, he had worked his way up to a very well-paid role in the automotive industry. He worked with senior executives at Fortune 500 companies, got paid to travel regularly, and lived in a beautiful house in Los Angeles. His life was good. By most standards, it was great, but something was missing for him. He just wasn't sure exactly what it was.

He says, "The irony of my predicament was that I was responsible for improving the performance of employees using the science of motivation. I had all of the knowledge, background, and tools to motivate hundreds of thousands of employees, but I could no longer motivate myself in my role. I was no longer being fulfilled. I was burning out, and my family life was suffering."

Then, a series of experiences made everything clear for him. He volunteered to travel to Africa to build a well that would provide clean water to a village there. When he saw the people in the village and how they struggled to have clean drinking water each day, it triggered something. He said, "Seeing how dramatic the need was, I knew I could no longer ignore it." He realized he could use his time and talent to make a more meaningful impact. He began to follow his passion by volunteering as a board member of Generosity.org. After months of consideration, he quit his corporate career to join the organization as the Executive Director. He traded his briefcase for a backpack—and traded success defined by money and status for success defined by service and purpose.

He told me it isn't easy to live in Los Angeles surrounded by the symbols of success and status that everyone recognizes. He says, "As adults, we learn to define success. As kids, we don't have these same definitions." He chose a new definition of success for himself, aligned with his values, rather than settle for the life everyone told him he should have.

* * *

While interviewing individuals about creating exceptional lives, I noticed three main reasons people accept good enough.

1) Commitment. I often talk to people who know they want something different, but they feel selfish for wanting it. They feel obligated to prioritize others' needs and desires over their own. Or they fall into the trap of believing that they are supposed to be a certain type of person, fulfilling the roles other people have defined for them. There are expectations of what success looks like, whether it be as a parent, child, partner, or employee. People often sacrifice their dreams for the sake of fulfilling these expectations, without questioning the sources. They may not even be aware that they have accepted other people's definitions and expectations as their own.

2) Comfort. At good enough, our needs are met. Life is comfortable in the specific ways that are important to us. Even people working long hours at jobs they hate have chosen a certain kind of comfort zone. They may not be happy, but they know what to expect. The results are predictable.

In his work, Victor consistently saw people who would occasionally take on a new challenge and push themselves slightly out of their comfort zone. They might learn a new language, pick up a hobby or start a sport. They would take on a new challenge for a while, but then it would become too uncomfortable and they would give up.

Victor explained, "People continue to do this throughout their lives, feeling as if they are making progress. There are peaks and valleys of accomplishment, but when you look at the through-line of results over the long-term, we end up leading an average life. We let our comfort zone stop us."

3) Confidence. Often, as we pursue a big goal or dream, we begin to doubt our own capabilities. I wrote this book because I saw so many talented and exceptional people stopping at good enough. They believed they weren't capable of having what they truly wanted. Somewhere along the way, they became convinced that more was not possible for them, and they accepted it. This form of settling for what is realistic can cause feelings of frustration and resentment. There is a constant nagging feeling that there must be more to life.

Our daily lives are demanding and busy. Each of these factors—commitment, comfort, and confidence—can quickly pull us back to good enough. Combined, they can have a powerful influence on our motivation and perspective. We believe that we can't pursue our dreams at the risk of everything else. Or can we? Many people from a wide variety of circumstances have been able to do just that.

* * *

Shelly overcame all three of these factors as she struggled to create the life she wanted for herself. As we talked, she told me how her life and career had followed the proven formula for success. She had gone to a good school, gotten good grades, and pursued a career in marketing. She was successfully climbing the ladder with some of the biggest agencies until she decided to put her career on hold in order to prioritize starting a family. She continued to work on part-time contracts while focusing on raising her three small children. Her choice was intentional, but it created an identity crisis for her. She didn't feel as though she was being her best in either role.

It was important to her to be there for her kids, but she wasn't happy being a stay-at-home mom. She was trying to balance her career and family in a way that was continually frustrating. She described her dilemma: "One week I thought, my most important task this week is to take brownies to the mom's group." She was fully present for her kids, but that was only a part of who she wanted to be and what she wanted to contribute to the world.

She continued, "On the other side of it, the next week I'd be gone for a marketing event and not available for my family." When she was traveling for work, she felt selfish for wanting to pursue a career that challenged her, at the expense of time with her husband and children.

When she found a job as a part-time marketing analyst, she believed she had found a better way to balance the two. The work gave her more flexibility to be at home rather than traveling for work and was aligned with her career goals. She thought she had solved the problem, but her new boss kept her in a very narrowly defined role. There was no room for growth. Shelly said, "It almost broke me. I lost my confidence and thought I couldn't do any better. I thought that working there was the best I could do." She was miserable. She felt trapped and didn't have the confidence to leave. She said, "As I was, I felt I wouldn't be worth much to anyone else."

Then, one day driving to work, the inspiration to change her situation came from an unlikely place—something she heard on the radio. Years later, she can still describe every detail of that moment. An employee at Tiger Stadium, the baseball stadium in her city, described how much he loved his job because he got to support his favorite team and eat healthy food from Subway.

Something about it hit her, and she thought to herself, "Where could I work that I could feel that passionate and love the work I was doing?"

Shelly realized that she needed to rebuild her confidence and find a different solution. After that day, she made several decisions that went contrary to all the conventional guidance. She sacrificed even more time with her kids to go back to school in the evenings for her MBA. She took a risk to invest some of the money set aside for her kids' college tuition in her own education. And, after receiving her degree, she took a huge career step "backward," accepting an intern-level role in an industry she knew she wanted to work in.

Only six months later, she was promoted to a management-level position with the Detroit Pistons. She completely reinvented her professional life. In the process, she found that she relates better to her kids and is also serving as a role model for them.

Shelly realized it is possible to create her own path, and she is looking toward the next stage of her journey.

She told me, "I don't think my story is done yet."

She was right, only a few months after we spoke, Shelly became Vice President of Strategy and Consulting at MMR LIVE Experience Design, a research consultancy focused on her passion—customer experience. Seven years after deciding to follow her own path, this role is the culmination of her efforts to build her confidence, build a network of supporters, and create the life she wanted.

Choosing your own definition of the life you want rather than accepting someone else's definition of "good enough" is the first step in creating an exceptional life. People who do this are often misunderstood by their friends, family, and colleagues, but they don't let that hold them back. They have clarity about what is important to them, and they pursue a version of success that is aligned with their values.

As I dug deeper into the stories of people who follow an unconventional path to success, I found that there are some specific ways they overcome the typical traps that keep others stuck.

LET GO OF DEFINITIONS

Shelly described the challenges she experienced in believing what might be possible. At each stage, she had to find a new perspective in her definition of herself. She had to become comfortable with a career transition from being a marketing executive to being a student again in her mid-forties, and then to being an intern in a new industry.

She slowly changed her definition of what it meant to be a good mother. Instead of defining it as being constantly available for sports practice and weekly parents' meetings, she redefined it as setting a strong example for her children by pursuing challenging goals.

She says, "You have to 'get over' who you think you are and where you think you fit." When we hold onto definitions of ourselves, often given to us by other people, we limit our potential to be something else.

Victor expressed a similar sentiment as he described his sudden transition from a sales executive dining in Michelin-star restaurants to someone traveling to remote villages in Africa, where clean water wasn't even available. He had to reconsider how he defined himself in the world, while he was still surrounded by people who measured success differently. He realized that it was more important to define himself by what he was contributing to others, rather than the car he drove or the restaurants where he ate.

LEVEL UP THE COMFORT ZONE

The only way to accomplish a new goal is to stay uncomfortable long enough to reach it. No one likes to be uncomfortable, but taking a different perspective makes it easier. The exceptions consistently choose short-term discomfort over long-term dissatisfaction. Each time they overcome discomfort in order to achieve a goal, it raises the comfort zone. Victor described it as "building habits that help us in the long-term to achieve slow and intentional progress."

Victor's point about slow and intentional progress is important. You don't grow by staying in your comfort zone, but you don't want to jump so far out of your comfort zone that you are terrified and paralyzed. There is an optimal zone for learning growth in the middle, which Russian psychologist Lev Vygotsky called the Zone of Proximal Development.[50]

For long-term progress, focus on the incremental steps you can take toward your goal. Stepping out of your comfort zone just far enough and long enough to achieve the goal creates new confidence and comfort. What was once challenging, now becomes normal, and your comfort zone expands.[51] Doing this regularly has a cumulative effect. It is a bit like advancing to the next level of a sport. When you are learning to play, it feels hard. After a few months of practice, the basics of the game come easily and naturally. You've mastered those skills and you can move to the next level.

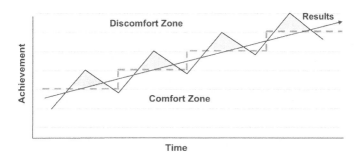

Shelly described how each step of her journey was uncomfortable for her. She was a student again, taking courses with people half her age. She had given up a well-paid management

50 Danny Iny, "What Science Says About Going Outside Your Comfort Zone," *Inc.*, November 8, 2016.
51 Ibid.

role and took an internship-level job to gain expertise in a new field. With each step, she built her confidence.

It wasn't only uncomfortable for her, but also for the people around her. While she was in school, she had less time for the children. Her mother-in-law and husband rearranged their schedules to help her. When she wanted to invest in her education and take a low-paying job as steps toward a new career, her husband supported the financial decisions and adjustments required. Rather than asking her to give up what was important to her to make their lives more comfortable, her family encouraged her to achieve her goals.

They recognized that in the long-term, her happiness and success was important for the success of the family. It even started to become evident to her children that she was an exception. One day, her daughter said to her, "Mom, I am starting to realize that you are not like all the other moms."

Shelly's story stands out because the people around her were also willing to temporarily step out of their own comfort zones to support her goals. Many people I spoke with described how, in the process of recreating their lives, they had to develop strategies to work around friends, family, or colleagues who insisted they should be satisfied with good enough.

KNOW WHEN SUPPORT ISN'T SUPPORTIVE

Our friends and family are generally concerned for our well-being. They want us to be safe, healthy, and happy. When we face challenges, they empathize with us and offer comforting words. This support is important in difficult moments, but it can also be the very thing that keeps us from reaching our goals. Sometimes, we are surrounded by people who not only give us permission to be mediocre; they encourage it.

While writing this book, I hit a creative and emotional wall several times. I couldn't find my way forward. I spent days struggling—spinning in circles about what I should do and wondering if I should just give up entirely and get a "real job." I reached out to friends and told them what I was thinking. As I listened to their advice, I realized something surprising. Everyone told me to stop trying so hard and be more realistic about my goals. I heard things like, "You are working too hard, you need to give yourself some time to slow down and take a holiday," or "Don't feel pressure to do so much, relax and go at your own pace." Somehow, taking it easy and waiting for the solution to fall at my feet didn't seem to make much sense.

I was feeling so stuck, that I reached out to a business coach. As I described my anxiety and frustration, she interrupted my complaining. She began, "These are challenging times for everyone, it is natural to feel anxiety. Give yourself time. It is okay if you don't accomplish all of your goals this year." She was repeating the advice I had gotten from my friends, *what you are doing is good enough—don't try so hard.*

In both cases, people were trying to boost my self-esteem. Their concerns were well-intended, but it felt like they were giving me permission to give up. In their attempts to be empathetic and supportive, they were telling me to go back to my comfort zone. I had everyone's permission to be comfortable and complacent.

We are sometimes overly critical of ourselves. However, there is a difference between being kind to ourselves and simply making excuses when we are uncomfortable. In these moments, the kind of support we receive is crucial. Many times, the people around us reinforce our own limiting beliefs and help us find the reasons something is not possible.

It becomes a vicious circle. You have a consensus that your doubts are justified and give up. This also allows the people around you to stay safely in their comfort zones. After all, if you accomplished something which they considered too difficult, they might have to reevaluate their own goals and perceptions.

People who accomplish exceptional things are careful about the opinions they accept. They seek a different kind of support. They have a knack for finding people that boost their confidence as they pursue new challenges, rather than people who tell them that everything is fine. They understand that change takes time, but they also surround themselves with people who remind them:

- they are capable
- discomfort is part of the process
- the goal is achievable

They stay focused on the person they want to become, and understand that temporary discomfort is better than long-term dissatisfaction. They work to expand their comfort zone step by step as they progress toward their own definition of success.

Being clear on the goal is the first step, but taking action isn't always easy. Victor and Shelly both carefully explored multiple options before making a change. The next chapters contain strategies to build confidence in the decision and successfully take action toward your goal.

SUMMARY

- Three things keep us stuck in a life that is "good enough": commitment, comfort, and lack of confidence.
- Definitions of success are often based on other people's opinions rather than our own values and goals.
- Overcome these blockers to an exceptional life by using these three strategies:
    - Let go of other people's definitions of what life should be and choose your own.
    - Make it easier to achieve goals by taking incremental steps outside your comfort zone to expand it gradually.
    - Seek support that empowers action rather than encourages complacency.

Clarity of Purpose

Overcome Expectations

Unapologetically Authentic

Return on Risk

Accelerate Action

Grow through Challenge

Embrace being Yourself

CHAPTER 6

RETHINK POSSIBLE

"Those who say it can't be done are usually interrupted by others doing it."

- JAMES BALDWIN

When we are little, we learn to color inside the lines.

It is one of the early developmental markers in young children, which usually occurs between ages three and five. Coloring inside the lines demonstrates fine motor skills and spatial recognition. According to Kimberly Williams, PsyD., a pediatric neuropsychologist, "the progression from scribbling to coloring inside the lines represents structure and rule following."[52]

After learning to color inside the lines, we are encouraged to make things the "right" colors. The sky is blue, the trees are green, and the sun is yellow. As we grow and learn, we are rewarded when we follow the rules and do the "right" things. It works well for parents, schools, and the community when we all play along and stick to the program. We are conditioned to conform.

We often forget, as adults, we can choose to color outside the lines again. Our potential to embrace our unique talents and ideas gets lost somewhere among the memorized textbook facts and ability to fill in ovals on a standardized test with a Number 2 pencil (staying inside the lines, of course). We can get so busy following the expected path that we lose sight of the options to explore new directions.

---

52 Kelsey Kloss, "The Magical Moment Your Pre-schooler Starts Coloring Inside the Lines," *Scholastic*, December 14, 2018.

STAYING IN THE LINES

Amy recalled, "I had a great life in New York, traveling business class, eating in the best restaurants, and even working for Google. To everyone else, my life seemed so put together, but I woke up every day not feeling happy, and I felt bad for feeling bad."

As the daughter of immigrant parents from a family-centric culture, Amy learned that a stable income and family should be her priorities. She studied hard, chose a solid career path, and successfully climbed the career ladder, working with prestigious brands like Booz Allen, Clorox, and Google. She had followed the rules and stayed inside the lines. And it had paid off.

By all usual definitions, she had an enviable life, but she felt stuck. She felt like she *should* be happy, but something felt off. She recalls, "I felt as though I was constantly behind in chasing the next thing I was supposed to go for."

She wanted something different. She wanted to quit her job and travel, but that felt like a huge risk. She struggled in silence because she had been taught to put on a "good face" and not share things going wrong. For months, she searched for answers but didn't find what she was looking for—the answer to the question "Do I settle and have babies or go live my dreams?"

The collection of *shoulds* in her head were relentless as she tried to make a decision, constantly reminding her:

- "You should be a good wife."

- "You should have babies because your eggs are rotting."
- "You should be grateful for what you have! You are such a spoiled brat."
- "You should be a good Chinese daughter and care for your parents, not go and play."
- "You should keep moving up the corporate ladder. It's safer."
- "You shouldn't be so stupid and give up everything you've worked so hard for."

Finally, out of pure desperation, she hired a coach. As part of their work together, Amy had created a vision board and, without being aware of it, she had written: "quit job." When the coach asked about it, Amy expressed her fear, "What if I quit, and I'm never able to make what I make now?" The coach asked a powerful question in reply, "Do you have to?"

She realized that everything she was afraid of—not making money, not being a responsible daughter and good wife—wasn't reflecting the reality of the situation. She became aware that there was more than one possible picture, and she could create one that matched her vision for her life.

Amy quit her job at Google. When I interviewed her, she and her husband had just volunteered for six months in Ghana while she launched a successful business. She now coaches women to "write their own story" just as she has done.

RETHINKING POSSIBLE

Larry Page, co-founder of Google, said in a commencement speech at University of Michigan that he had been "taught how to make dreams real" in a training program there called LeaderShape, whose slogan was to have "a healthy disregard for the impossible."[53] This disregard for the impossible is as valuable in the process of reinventing our own lives as it is for inventing new software or new methods of transportation. We first have to believe that there is a different way to reach the goal. We can only find a new solution or a new path by overcoming the expectations of the people who think that there isn't one. We have to unlearn what we believe to be true to discover other possibilities.

We work hard to gain knowledge and experience in order to make better decisions and achieve results. As we acquire more experience, we become confident in what we know. We reach a level of expertise, or we trust other experts, and we stop questioning the underlying assumptions. The impact of this certainty is often seen in industries that are slow to change and the assumptions they make. Kodak, whose business was based on printing photos, had digital photo technology but missed the opportunity to shift to digital photo sharing. They even owned one of the first photo-sharing platforms, Ofoto. Unfortunately, they used Ofoto to try to get more people to print images rather than share them.[54] Blockbuster was so preoccupied with its brick-and-mortar video rental stores that they didn't pursue the alternatives of video streaming or subscription services until it was much too late. They even passed up the opportunity to buy

53 Google: News from Google, "Larry Page's University of Michigan Commencement Address," May 2, 2009, video, 16:28.

54 Scott D. Anthony, "Kodak's Downfall wasn't about Technology," Harvard Business Review, July 15, 2016.

Netflix.[55] Both companies eventually filed for bankruptcy. Their expertise in the industries they once led blinded them to the shifting customer demands.

The problem with what we think we know is that it is based on the situation yesterday, a year ago, or ten years ago. Relying solely on expertise causes complacency. People with decades of experience believe they already have the answers and know what can be accomplished. They become comfortable with the status quo and fail to recognize alternate possibilities.

The world is changing quickly. The circumstances, technology, capabilities, and behaviors of the past are not necessarily an accurate foundation for making decisions today or tomorrow. I found that many people who accomplish exceptional results simply didn't know the "facts" that other people were certain of, or they at least questioned the assumptions. When they were told that what they wanted to accomplish wasn't possible, they refused to take no for an answer.

Kara Goldin is, by her own description, "an accidental entrepreneur." She is the Founder and CEO of Hint, Inc., known for Hint® water, the leading unsweetened flavored water.[56] She started the company to solve a problem in her own life. She was addicted to diet soda and wanted to start drinking more water, but she found plain water too boring. She started adding fruit to her water, and her friends started asking her

55 "The Rise and Fall of Blockbuster and How It's Surviving with Just One Store Left," *Business Insider,* August 12, 2020, video, 08:27.

56 Nikki Barua and Kara Goldin, "Episode 104: Overcoming Doubts and Doubters with Hint CEO Kara Goldin," in *Beyond Barriers,* podcast, audio, 42:46.

for it. She had no experience in the beverage industry, but she saw a need that wasn't being filled. She began creating healthy flavored water without artificial ingredients in her own kitchen.[57]

She hit a major roadblock early in the process. Her mission was to create a healthy alternative, not another sugary drink with lots of unrecognizable ingredients. She was unwilling to add sweeteners and preservatives to the water. This meant that the product had a very limited shelf-life, and, therefore, couldn't be widely distributed. She searched for a solution unsuccessfully but refused to give up. She decided to produce and deliver the flavored water locally, while continuing to search for a way to create a longer shelf-life without compromising her values.[58]

At one point in her research, she managed to speak with an executive at one of the world's largest beverage companies and asked for his insights. He interrupted her and told her no one would want the product. He was dismissive of the concept and the healthy results it was creating for people. She didn't listen and decided to prove him wrong.[59] Two years later, she and her husband found their own way to increase the shelf-life while keeping only natural ingredients.[60]

---

57 Kara Goldin, *Undaunted: Overcoming Doubts and Doubters* (New York: HarperCollins Leadership, 2020), Introduction, Kindle.

58 Ibid.

59 Ibid.

60 Kara Goldin, *Undaunted: Overcoming Doubts and Doubters* (New York: HarperCollins Leadership, 2020), Introduction, Kindle.

The industry experts said it couldn't be done, and yet two people with no experience did it. And they did it spectacularly. The company now has over $150 million in sales and is expanding into other healthy products.[61]

My theory is that they were able to do it specifically because they didn't have the "expertise" in the way it has always been done. They didn't know the rules of the game, so they weren't limited by them. The challenge of finding a solution was more important to them than the pressure to listen to the experts.

THE POWER OF CAN'T

Each of the people I interviewed expressed how much they enjoy a challenge. Most of them even sought out difficult goals on purpose. Several people described intentionally choosing difficult projects, even when there was no professional benefit to them, simply for the challenge of it. For these people, one of the strongest motivations to accomplish something is being told it can't be done. They'll most likely immediately set out to prove it is possible.

In his book, *Originals*, Adam Grant talks about a study regarding negotiating style. In the study, people who were told they were likely to win in a negotiation were actually less likely to succeed than the people who were told they were the underdog. It turned out that the people who were predicted to succeed got complacent, while the underdogs worked hard to prove the "expert" wrong.[62]

---

61   "My Story," Kara Goldin, accessed February 12, 2021.
62   *Adam Grant*, "WorkLife with Adam Grant: The Creative Power of Misfits," March 2019, TED podcast, audio, 40:17.

Grant goes on to explore how telling people that they cannot achieve something can inspire them to succeed. The difference in motivation comes down to whether they believe the person evaluating their ability is credible or not and also how much it is in alignment with their beliefs about themselves. If the person questioning their ability is perceived as the enemy (management, for example) this doubt can actually drive people to succeed, just to prove the enemy wrong.[63]

Remember, expectations are powerful predictors of the results we get, but only if we accept those expectations as true. If the expectation is out of alignment with our belief about ourselves, it can actually serve as a catalyst. Or at the very least, an annoyance that we ignore, while we are busy accomplishing the thing that everyone says we cannot.

In Shelly's case, the frustration with her manager that refused to give her opportunities to grow eventually became the "can't" that drove her to prove herself in a new career. Most people who pursue an unconventional path have been told by friends or colleagues that their goal was crazy or impossible. And consistently, they all listened, nodded politely, and then did it anyway.

I have experienced this phenomenon several times in my life. I found that the more my friends and family doubted me, the harder I worked to prove them wrong. Once I announced I was going to achieve something, failing to accomplish it was simply not an option. I remember a specific conversation with a respected acquaintance in Los Angeles. We

---

63 Ibid.

were having breakfast at a cozy little diner in my neighborhood and discussing business strategy. He was the CEO and founder of a technology company with millions in annual revenues, and I valued his advice and business expertise.

My business was growing slowly. I had just brought on additional employees and announced that this year, I would double my revenues. The year was 2008, and we were in the midst of the biggest recession I'd seen in my career. He was quick to point this out, and said, "There is no way that you can double your sales in a recession." He also emphasized that, especially in the automotive industry, which were my primary clients, I'd be lucky to even retain current accounts.

His rationale wasn't without logic. The automotive industry had been hit hard by the recession and was in crisis. Two of the big three US manufacturers had already requested emergency loans and, in early 2009, would require a massive government bailout to avoid bankruptcy. I took a sip of my coffee, looked across the table, and told him that he was too focused on the problem rather than the opportunity. I think I even said, "I'll prove that you are wrong."

That year, not only did I achieve the goal of doubling my sales revenues, I tripled them. You see, even though his company was ten times more successful than mine, he didn't understand my business. I knew that the industry would need consultants more than ever to find ways to operate more efficiently. And they would no longer be able to afford the big expensive agencies with slow turnaround and high margins. My company was small and nimble. We operated lean and had incredibly low overhead, which meant we could accomplish results faster at a lower price than our biggest competitors.

It wasn't easy. I had to learn to scale quickly, overcome my resistance to cold calls and traditional sales pitches, and get creative about our positioning in the market. But I knew that no matter what it took, I couldn't let his opinion of what I was capable of accomplishing be the deciding factor in my success.

DRAW YOUR OWN PICTURE

The things you *should* do are formed from other people's beliefs, experiences, and opinions. Accepting these *shoulds* without questioning their truth allows someone else to draw the picture for your life. You might be able to use sparkly colors to make the picture seem perfect, but it is still not your masterpiece. The best you can do by coloring inside the lines is to have a beautiful version of someone else's picture of life.

There is value in the lessons we learn as children, and even as adults. But having only one possible picture limits our experience and our results. If we believe that trees must be green, we miss the joy of a palette of brilliant autumn reds, oranges, and yellows. Just because something is usually one way, doesn't mean there aren't other possibilities.

The way other people have done something is not necessarily the best way, or the only way, to do it. We can create new paradigms, go outside the lines, and find a new path. If we spend our entire lives doing what we *should* do, we will never know what new pictures we could create.

The people that accomplish exceptional results in their lives believe that exceptional results are possible. They believe they are capable of achieving their dream and creating their own masterpiece. And the amazing thing is... they are right.

People who create new solutions succeed in part because of their willingness to challenge the way it is usually done and go outside the lines. In the next chapter, we'll explore the mindset that creates the confidence to stand out.

SUMMARY

- The things we believe we *should* do are often defined by other people and are not aligned with what we want for ourselves.
- We can do things differently and create our own picture of the life we want to live.
- Expertise can limit the ability to see new opportunities outside of the lines.
- Expectations are only predictors of our results if we accept them as true.
- New solutions come from seeing problems from a different perspective and challenging those who say it can't be done.

Clarity of Purpose

Overcome Expectations

Unapologetically Authentic

Return on Risk

Accelerate Action

Grow through Challenge

Embrace being Yourself

CHAPTER 7

REJECT NORMAL

———

"If you are always trying to be normal, you will never know how amazing you can be."

- MAYA ANGELOU

As I was procrastinating one day, desperately trying to avoid my German language lessons, I stumbled across a TEDx Talk entitled, "'Good' and 'Bad' are Incomplete Stories We Tell Ourselves," and I clicked play.[64] The topic wasn't at all what I expected. The speaker was Heather Lanier. She is the mother of a child born with a rare genetic disease, which results in severe developmental challenges. She captured her experiences in her book, *Raising a Rare Girl*, and questions our assumptions about "good" and "bad." She challenges us to stop fixating on solutions for whatever we deem not normal and embrace our differences.[65]

She told the story of her early experiences with the doctors and therapists who were trying to help her daughter, Fiona, in the first years of her life. She says, "We had a few therapists visit our house that first year, and they usually focused on what was bad about my kid."[66]

She goes on to give an example of how Fiona's tiny fingers were crumpled into odd curves due to the disease. The therapists considered this bad because her hands were not shaped like "normal" hands. One therapist suggested devising a splint, which Lanier explains "would rob my kid of the ability to actually use those fingers, but it would at least force them into some position that looked normal."[67] Fiona had already started using her hands to interact and learn about the world around her, and Lanier questioned the logic.

---

64 Heather Lanier, "Good and Bad are Incomplete Stories We Tell Ourselves," filmed October 2017 in Milan, Italy, TED video, 13:28.

65 Ibid.

66 Ibid.

67 Ibid.

As she struggled with how best to help her daughter, she began to challenge the underlying assumptions. She says, "I could believe that the good path was the path that erased as many differences as possible. Of course, this would have been a disastrous pursuit, because at the cellular level, my daughter had rare blueprints."[68]

After listening to this story, I wondered, why are we so focused on being "normal"? The truth is that we all have rare blueprints—that is the reason that no two fingerprints are alike. What is it then that causes us to focus so much of our attention and energy on fitting in to what is normal rather than standing out as different? Why is being different so "bad" that we actively sacrifice or hide what makes us unique?

FITTING IN

I realized that I had experienced this in my own life in a much less dramatic way. I am a bit shy with rather average physical characteristics, making it fairly easy for me to blend in my whole life. I never even thought about all the ways I was subtly making decisions to fit in until I moved to Germany in 2015.

The move was sudden and completely unplanned—I had prepared to live in Spain. I didn't speak a word of German, didn't know anyone in the country, and was unfamiliar with the culture. As part of adapting to my new life, I wanted to integrate quickly. I found a language tutor before I even

---

68 Ibid.

had a place to live. I bought books, read blogs, and tried to learn as much about my new surroundings and culture as possible. How hard could it be? After all, Germany is a western, industrialized country, which has been significantly influenced by the United States.

After two years of struggling to fit in and being unsuccessful, I was frustrated, lonely, and depressed. I was meeting people regularly and, at this stage, even having conversations in German, but I couldn't seem to make close friends. What was I doing wrong? Why was it so hard? I began to doubt myself and looked at other areas of my life for clues. I had made many new friends in Spain, France, and England, but Germany continued to be a challenge.

One day, while walking back from lunch with a German colleague, I asked a question about the proper etiquette when meeting new people. This particular topic constantly perplexed me in Europe—do I shake hands or kiss them on each cheek, do I address them formally or informally? As I expressed how nervous I was about meeting people, simply because I didn't know how to greet them, my colleague said something that changed everything.

He stopped in the middle of the sidewalk, looked directly at me and said, "Vicki, why are you trying so hard to fit in? No matter what you do, you will not be German. Your unique advantage is that you are American and bring a different perspective. People appreciate the difference. Why are you trying to hide that and be like everyone else? Be yourself."

The statement hit me like a lightning bolt. All this time, I was trying so hard to fit in that I wasn't being authentic. I had become less vocal, less confident in expressing ideas, and less interesting. I couldn't make friends in Germany because people never actually got to know *me*. I was hiding my naturally curious personality, my strong style of communicating, and my rather dry sense of humor.

I made friends easily in other countries because I didn't make an effort to fit in. In those countries, I was only visiting for a few days, so there was no pressure to impress anyone or even to build any long-term relationships. I wasn't concerned about what people thought and could easily be my outspoken, energetic self. In contrast, when adapting to my new home in Germany, I was so worried about making the "right" impression that I had bent myself into an unrecognizable pretzel. I was trying to be something that I simply couldn't be, no matter how good my acting or language skills.

I thought I was doing the right thing by attempting to conform to the community that I had become a part of. It backfired because instead of simply showing courtesy and respect for cultural differences, I had completely lost myself in trying to fit in and be "normal" in my new environment.

THE ADVANTAGES OF NORMAL

I wondered how I had so easily missed this simple distinction. I had fallen victim to the "acceptance" *shoulds*. We are socialized to fit in when we are young, and I had unconsciously carried these associated behaviors into situations where they no longer helped me.

Belonging is one of our basic human needs and our brain is wired to make sure that we are accepted in our community. Hundreds of years ago, it was important to be accepted in order to survive. The community ensured that we had food and were protected from predators or intruders. Even now, being liked and accepted still impacts the opportunities we have, our self-esteem, and the resources available to us. Our society has a set of rules and systems that have become the norm, and we are conditioned to follow them.

Observing my nieces and nephews over the past years, I saw that this desire to fit in developed as they grew. I can recall when my nieces were very young, they loved playing dress-up. They had princess dresses, funny hats, and super-hero capes. My nephew had a pair of cowboy boots that he wore everywhere, despite his mother's embarrassment. In kindergarten and first grade, the kids loved to go to school in their favorite costumes. It never occurred to them that it wasn't completely appropriate to go to school as Snow White or Batman. They wore what made them happy and expressed their dreams.

As they got older, this quickly changed. Suddenly, they wanted a different kind of costume. Now they came home from school begging to go shopping because they needed the trendy brand of jeans or the latest sneakers. They were horrified if they were asked to wear something that their older brother or sister had worn a year earlier. They were desperate to wear the most popular brands and styles, and rational arguments about cost were met with, "But if I have to wear that, I'll die!"

The desire to be like everyone else wasn't, and isn't, limited to clothes. Now that they are teenagers, there is daily bargaining over how to get the latest iPhone, Apple Watch, or whatever it is that everyone has now. It seems as if there is a giant race to be the fastest and the best at being just like everyone else.

Of course, we aren't only susceptible as teenagers to this race to fit in. I also see examples of this every day with my corporate clients. As a specialist in training, I work regularly with small teams across various departments and companies. I often notice that the teams are largely homogeneous. The people on any particular team tend to have similar backgrounds in education, origin, and experience. When I asked the managers about why they selected specific people for their team, the response generally sounded something like, "We had a few candidates that were well-qualified, but Susan just seemed to fit in better with the team culture."

What often happens with these teams is that they struggle to innovate because everyone has similar experiences and perspectives. There is no resource to challenge the norm or offer fresh ideas. I had one client that recognized this and started doing something differently with great results. They were in the business of selling cars, and they had always hired experienced salespeople. But the industry was very competitive, and they had trouble retaining staff. So, instead of hiring experienced "car guys," they started hiring women with no sales or automotive experience. What happened next surprised everyone. The employees without sales experience listened to customers more carefully and asked more questions because they didn't assume they had all the answers. Both profit margin and customer satisfaction went up because customers felt listened to rather than sold to. Sometimes all it takes is a different perspective.

We can all feel pressure throughout our careers to fit in, and we play along. Think about the last time you started a new job. Did you wear the clothes you felt most confident in, or did you adapt your wardrobe to fit the "uniform" of your new team? Would you go to work at a tech start-up wearing a suit? Would you go to a corporate banking job wearing a t-shirt and jeans? Most people would not be so bold, and those that are might not have that job very long. Fitting in serves the purpose of making the people around us comfortable and setting certain expectations for our behavior. It makes our routine interactions feel normal and less stressful.

It is not just about clothes—you can see the natural inclination for acceptance in all aspects of life. Think about the last meeting you attended with senior level executives. Did you withhold an idea or opinion because it was contrary to the opinion of the senior person in the room? Did you adjust your personality to be more assertive or more deferential? In subtle ways, we do all sorts of things every day in an attempt to fit in and gain approval.

Of course, there are some advantages to fitting in. Acceptance, opportunity, status, and lack of conflict are just a few. People are able to relate to us more easily. They don't feel threatened by behaviors or opinions which they don't understand. We don't cause discomfort at company meetings or dinner parties. People like us because we are like them, and that makes us feel better about ourselves.

But do these advantages really outweigh the disadvantages? As I learned from my colleague, sometimes in our pursuit of "fitting in" or being "normal," we limit the very characteristics that enable us to succeed in contributing to the world.

THE DANGERS OF NORMAL

In order to solve problems and create new solutions, we need the courage to express unique perspectives, vocalize fresh ideas, and discuss opposing concepts. If we are all trying to fit in, then that leaves us stuck with the status quo. Until we begin to question what is "normal," nothing can change. Remember at one point, not very long ago, it was normal for women to stay at home with the kids while their husbands worked. And it was normal to look things up in an encyclopedia, listen to music on CDs, and communicate with people by sending a piece of paper across the country with a stamp on it.

We are now seeing more and more data to make the case for standing out rather than fitting in. For example, a 2018 study of thousand companies across twelve countries by McKinsey and Co. found that companies in the top quartile for gender diversity on their executive teams were 21 percent more likely to experience above-average profitability.[69] Research also shows that ethnic and cultural diversity resulted in a 33 percent increase in performance.[70]

In his book, *The Diversity Bonus*, Scott Page makes a compelling case for teams made of up people who are different from

---

69 Vivian Hunt et al., *Delivering through Diversity* (McKinsey & Company, 2018), 1.
70 Ibid.

each other, and therefore, think differently. He points out that differences in how people think are what enable teams to develop more creative solutions, make fewer errors, and construct more accurate predictions than individuals.[71]

If research proves that expressing different ideas and embracing diversity creates better solutions and more profitable companies, why do we still feel so much pressure to fit in?

There is some comfort in what we deem as "normal." At least, when we are striving to be normal or fit in, the goal is clear. We can see examples all around us of what to imitate. The media tells us what we should wear, what we should eat, and what we should buy to be part of the "in" crowd. Fitting in is in many ways easier. It gives us a feeling of belonging and makes us more confident in our decisions because they are the same as everyone else's decisions and opinions.

The problem is that we make worse decisions and are less likely to contribute anything truly unique to the community. In addition, constantly striving to be something we are not can be extremely exhausting. Everything becomes an act, and we can feel like an impostor in our own lives. At some point, it is simply no longer sustainable.

I met Nikki fifteen years ago in Southern California. At the time, she and I were competing for business with my biggest client. Her agency was new to the scene, but,

---

71   Scott E. Page, *The Diversity Bonus: How Great Teams Pay Off in the Knowledge Economy* (New Jersey: Princeton University Press, 2017), Introduction.

admittedly, offered solutions in technology that my team simply couldn't. I was impressed with her and how quickly she grew her business. She was a powerful presence in a room, confident, charismatic, and obviously extremely capable at her work. I was in awe of what she had achieved.

What I didn't know at the time was that Nikki was putting so much pressure on herself that she was barely holding it together. Years before, she had come to the US from India and immediately felt like an outsider. She needed to integrate quickly, and she carefully watched and imitated the people around her. Now she describes it this way: "I wanted so badly to fit in, that I got caught up in comparison, but the more I was like everyone else, the less there was of me."[72]

I have heard this sentiment from more colleagues and friends than I can count. They get caught up in the pressure to fit in, and they focus on comparisons to the people around them. They become so busy doing all the "right" things that they lose track of why they are pushing themselves so hard. Eventually, some event in their lives forces them to pause for a moment. When they do, they look at their life and wonder how they "lost themselves" along the way.

Nikki was one of those people that was finally forced to pause. A series of traumatic events, coupled with the constant pressure to succeed, eventually took its toll. Her health suffered, and she experienced a period of severe burnout and depression. After hitting such a low point, she realized, "I had to choose a

---

72   Nick Stagge and Nikki Barua, "This is Nikki Barua," April 29, 2020, in *The Ordinary* podcast, audio, 53:57.

path that was congruent to my beliefs[...] I no longer had the desire to subscribe to conventional beliefs or the conventional way of doing things[...] It liberated me to be fully me."[73]

In many ways, striving to be normal and achieve conventional definitions of success keeps us in our comfort zone, or at least, the comfort zone of those around us. However, it often creates a disconnect between the person we show to the world and our authentic selves. It causes us to hide our differences, exhaust our emotions, and deprive our communities of our unique gifts.

EXCEPTIONS DO THINGS DIFFERENTLY

Here's the thing. We are conditioned by society and culture to follow the rules and systems. We are led to believe that the path to greatness is predictable and linear, like an athlete that trains day after day, year after year for the Olympics. We are taught that there is a formula. If you follow the right steps, in the right order, and listen to the experts, you too can achieve great success.

However, in many cases, the people that we perceive as truly great didn't follow the proven formula. They didn't follow advice from the experts. In fact, they did exactly the opposite! They ignored the advice. They overcame the trends and the pressure to fit in, and they did it their way. And that is exactly what led to their success—they were the exception.

---

73 Ibid.

Will Smith is a powerful Hollywood A-lister and has been ranked as one of the most bankable stars worldwide.[74] But he didn't set out to be an actor. He knew from a young age that he wanted to be a rapper and passed up opportunities to go to college. When he began rapping, he didn't like the profanity and aggression that was typical for rap at the time. So, he created his own style, infused with storytelling and light-hearted humor. It stood out because his brand of rap was completely different than everyone around him.[75]

It was this unique style that made him an instant hit when he partnered with DJ Jazzy Jeff. When his music career hit a slump, he got the unexpected opportunity for a role on a new TV sitcom. Even though he had never acted and had no training, he knew he couldn't pass up the opportunity.[76] The role in the show, *Fresh Prince of Bel Air,* changed the course of his career, opening the way to become one of the world's most successful actors. If he had started out trying to follow the "normal" path to acting success, the story might have ended much differently.

Another wildly successful entertainer who didn't follow the proven path to success is Eddie Murphy. Eddie started out doing stand-up comedy with a dirty and edgy style that was definitely not the norm. Around age seventeen or eighteen, he was playing at the Comic Strip in Fort Lauderdale on the same night that Rodney Dangerfield was headlining. He was bold enough to ask Dangerfield for his opinion of his

---

74 "The Numbers Bankability Index," The Numbers, accessed March 2, 2021.
75 "Will Smith Biography," Biography, updated January 8, 2021.
76 Rebbekah Wiltons, "The Fascinating Life Story of Will Smith," *Worldation* (blog), October 16, 2018.

routine. Dangerfield answered, "I don't know where you're gonna go with that, you know? The language, and the race stuff." Eddie was crestfallen, but he didn't change his style. Two or three years later, after he was a success on *Saturday Night Live*, the two met again. Dangerfield shrugged and said, "Who knew?"[77]

The common thread in the success stories I hear is that the person trusted their own instincts and values. They were confident in who they were, and they didn't change it to fit in with the crowd. They didn't listen to advice from experts about the way it should be done or look for the fast formula to check the boxes for success. They did it differently. And they achieved success specifically because they stood out from the crowd.

In an interview on success strategies, Annie Jean-Baptiste, Head of Product Inclusion at Google, admits that we all struggle with trying to fit in at times, especially in career situations. But she points out that we need to embrace what makes us different. In describing her own career, she says, "The stuff that made me different was actually my ability to add value." She goes on to point out that it is important to figure out what makes you unique and utilize it. In her words, "You don't have to be good at everything—you just need to be great at one thing."[78]

77 *W Magazine*, "Eddie Murphy on the Worst Advice He Received," January 20, 2020, video, 4:38.

78 Annie Jean-Baptiste and Monica Marquez, "Episode 69: How Your Authenticity Fuels Innovation with Google's Annie Jean-Baptiste," in *Beyond Barriers*, podcast, audio, 35:57.

Imagine a world where we stopped assuming that normal is "good" and different is "bad." How much could we accomplish if instead of pouring our energy into fitting in and being normal, we spent our time discovering our uniqueness and standing out? After all, no significant changes have ever come from agreeing with the majority or doing what everyone else was doing. Change comes from having the courage to do something differently.

Doing things differently is often seen as a risk. The next chapter uncovers how changing the perspective on risk can make it easier to pursue bold goals.

SUMMARY

- As children, we learn that "normal" is good and "different" is bad—we are socialized to fit in.
- Belonging is one of our basic human needs, and fitting in makes it easier to feel safe and secure.
- Adapting to what people around us expect stifles our unique perspective and results in homogeneous groups and decisions.
- Each person is unique, with characteristics and talents that set us apart. We are most successful when we embrace and use these gifts.

Clarity of Purpose

Overcome Expectations

Unapologetically Authentic

Return on Risk

Accelerate Action

Grow through Challenge

Embrace being Yourself

CHAPTER 8

RECONSIDER RISK

"Only those who will risk going too far can possibly find out how far one can go."

- T.S. ELIOT

"You can choose to climb a mountain on your hands and knees. You might eventually get to the top, but it will certainly take longer and be more painful." This is the way a friend described her perspective on risk. Climbing on your hands and knees is "safer" because you'd be less likely to fall, but it is certainly not effective. It is a ridiculous example, but it made me stop and think about how many times in our lives we make flawed assumptions about risk which impact our decisions. How many times do we crawl toward our goals, rather than walking confidently ahead, because we believe that is the safest way to get there?

Nothing in life is without risk. Every decision comes with the potential for either a positive or negative outcome. We each take hundreds of risks every day—driving to the office, getting on an airplane, crossing the street, going to the gym, eating a piece of fish for dinner—any one of these activities has the potential to result in injury or death... and yet, we still do them. Even walking is risky. According to the CDC, over one million Americans are injured each year in slip and fall accidents, and more than seventeen thousand of those accidents result in death.[79]

The problem is that we forget that everything we do is a choice, and everything has a risk. Our awareness of risk in daily activities decreases as they become routine and have predictable outcomes. Our brain develops shortcuts, which help us process information and make decisions more quickly. If every action required a risk evaluation, we would be constantly overwhelmed with worry and would have

---

79 "Slip and Fall Accident Stats," Lawfirms.com, accessed February 12, 2021.

trouble getting out of bed in the morning. It is not possible to avoid risk completely. The key to more success is understanding how we identify and evaluate potential risks and make decisions about which risks we take.

RETURN ON RISK

Ask any athlete, executive, musician, or entrepreneur, and I would bet that you learn that none of them achieved their success by playing it safe. Somewhere along the way, they all took a chance and risked security for success. James Dyson, who invented Dyson vacuums, spent five years working on his idea, had taken three mortgages on his house, and created over five thousand prototypes before he created the winning design. He now has a net worth of $1.6 billion.[80] J.K. Rowling was a single mother and as close to broke as possible without being homeless, but she continued to write and pursue her goal, even after being rejected by multiple publishers.[81]

Richard Branson sums it up perfectly when he explains, "In the end, you have to take calculated risks; otherwise you are going to sit in mothballs all day and do nothing."[82]

If deciding to take a risk is a choice, either consciously or subconsciously, then how can we get smarter about the risks we choose to take so that we are more likely to reach our goals?

---

80 "In Pictures: The Greatest Risk They Ever Took: James Dyson," Interviewed by Matthew Kirdahy in 2008, *Forbes,* January 21, 2010.

81 Year on Team, "Failure. Rejection. Success: The J.K. Rowling Story," *Year On* (blog), January 15, 2015.

82 Lisa Ocker, "Business Branson Style," *Success* (blog), April 30, 2008.

In business, most large strategy decisions are made based on the return on investment (ROI). This is especially true for things that require larger investments of time and money. ROI is used to determine whether to build a new retail location, invest in research for a new product, or decide whether it is worth it to spend millions on an advertisement during the Superbowl.

The basic formula for evaluating return on investment is:

ROI = total revenue generated minus total cost invested / total cost of the investment

Of course, there are other important factors that can affect ROI decisions. For example, the time needed to generate the profit means that resources are not available for other potential investments during that same time period. This is the opportunity cost.

For example, if you invest $100 in a stock today and sell it one year later for $120, your return on investment is 20 percent. However, if you could invest that same $100 today in creating a product that you could sell next month for $120, your return on investment would still be 20 percent, but you would have the money more quickly to make additional new investments. The estimation of both future returns and the value of missed opportunities is one of the trickiest parts of evaluating potential ROI because neither is guaranteed.

In my experience, I notice that many people make decisions about new opportunities in their lives, much like calculating a personal ROI, by subconsciously calculating the "Return on Risk." However, for these more personal decisions, we tend to be more emotional and aren't very scientific in our calculations. We also add factors to the equation that our brains simply aren't very good at estimating. These factors lead us to make inaccurate decisions about the possibility of success, especially when it requires more time to achieve the goal and the results are further in the future.

Let's start with a familiar example. From a mathematical perspective, everyone knows (or should know) that playing the lottery is a terrible investment. Your chances of winning the New York Powerball would be 1 in 292 million.[83] The chance of getting hit by lightning in any given year (1 in 500,000)[84] or becoming a movie star (1 in 1.5 million)[85] is much better. If buying a lottery ticket has such a terrible return on investment, why do so many people do it?

The short answer is that even though odds are against us, the risk is so small and the payoff so immediate, that we convince ourselves it still has a good potential Return on Risk.

Based on the conversations I've had with people who are considering a major life change (new job, new home, or new business, as an example), the factors they weigh in their decisions are closely aligned with a typical ROI formula and include

---

83 "Odds and Prizes," New York Lottery, New York State Gaming Commission, accessed February 12, 2021.

84 "Lightning: Victim Data," Centers for Disease Control and Prevention, accessed February 12, 2021.

85 Buzzfeed, "The Chances of You Being Famous," February 11, 2014, video, 1:49.

four main considerations. Each person gives more weight to some considerations than others, but they generally include:

Reward:	What do I gain if the result is successful?
Relevance:	How important is the result to me? How likely is success?
Risk:	What investment is required (financial, emotional, and personal effort)?
Result Timeline:	How quickly can I get the result, and what must I give up or miss out on?

In the case of the lottery, the reward is very high, even though the likelihood of a winning result is low. The risk and required effort are also very low, and the result is immediate. There is a lot to gain and almost nothing to lose, so we take the chance.

Another example of a risk which most of us take every day is driving to work. We know that people are injured or die in car accidents, but we still get in our cars and drive to the office.

Why is that risk so easy to take that we barely notice? Let's look at the factors:

Reward:	I get to keep my job, which provides income for my family.
Relevance:	It is very important, and success is almost certain (arriving at the office).
Risk:	Thirty minutes in traffic, cost of gas/maintenance, chance of an accident
Result Timeline:	Immediate with little missed opportunity, except thirty minutes extra sleep or personal time

In this case, both the reward and the relevance are very high, and the results are immediate. We know there is a risk, but the reward is more important to us and also seems likelier than the possible danger, which feels rare.

ERRORS IN RISK CALCULATION

So far, our decisions seem pretty logical. The challenge comes when we evaluate more complex risks or larger opportunities in our lives, such as changing jobs or starting a business. These kinds of risks occur less frequently, and, therefore, have more unknown components, which we attempt to estimate. The problem is that in these types of decisions, we have several cognitive biases which can impact our judgment of the potential risk versus the possible reward.

Cognitive biases are systematic patterns in processing and interpreting information from the world around us, which affect judgment and decision-making. Generally, cognitive biases help us to process information and make decisions for routine activities faster and easier. However, we often make predictable errors in the way we interpret or perceive the information in comparison to the actual data.[86]

Here are just two ways that biases can affect our judgment, which could explain why we might play the lottery but be unwilling to gamble on our own success.

---

86 Kendra Cherry, "What is Cognitive Bias," *Verywell Mind*, July 19, 2020.

COGNITIVE BIAS #1: LIKELIHOOD OF AN EVENT

Research done by noted psychologist and economist, Daniel Kahneman, with Amos Tversky, found that people estimate the frequency of an event based on the ease with which it comes to mind, known as the availability heuristic. The awareness we have of something causes bias when we estimate the likelihood that a particular event will occur.[87]

For example, when making an assessment of how likely you are to have a car accident, chances are you don't look up the insurance statistics for accidents in your city. Instead, you think about the people you know who have had a car accident. Recent examples, or more emotional ones, are weighted more heavily because you have a stronger awareness of them.[88] If a colleague is out of work because they had a car accident yesterday, you may be more cautious about driving today because that information is top of mind.

Of course, it doesn't have to be a personal experience. It can also be information you've collected from news or other media. Because exciting events are more likely to be publicized than common and boring events, these dramatic exceptions are easier to bring to mind and, therefore, seem more likely to occur.[89]

What this means in practice is that you make decisions based primarily on the information you have collected, whatever the source. You are much more likely to see news stories

---

87 Daniel Kahneman, *Thinking, Fast and Slow* (London: Penguin Random House, 2012), 129-138.
88 Ibid.
89 Ibid.

about excited lottery winners than reports on all of the millions of people who have lost. This awareness causes the probability of winning to seem greater than it truly is from the perspective of your brain.

COGNITIVE BIAS #2: OVERESTIMATING RISK AND UNDERESTIMATING REWARD

Not only does our brain give more weight to information that is easily memorable or accessible, but it also prioritizes perceived threats above possible opportunities.[90] Our brain is designed for survival, and that means its primary goal is to keep us alive and safe. In order to stay safe, we unconsciously give more attention to things considered a threat. According to Kahneman, in *Thinking, Fast and Slow*, potential gains are a reward, while potential losses are perceived as a threat. We are naturally inclined toward loss aversion. When potential losses are weighed against possible gains, "losses loom larger than gains."[91]

To add to this conundrum, we have a tendency for confirmation bias, which means we seek information which supports what we already believe.[92] We subconsciously seek to prove ourselves right. So, if you believe the common statement that half of all new businesses fail in the first year (which is incorrect), you will focus on all the examples you find of failed businesses. This increased awareness means that examples of failed entrepreneurs are more easily available

---

90 Kahneman, *Thinking, Fast and Slow*, 282-284.
91 Ibid.
92 *Encyclopedia Britannica*, s.v. "Confirmation Bias," October 9, 2019.

in your thoughts and creates a vicious circle convincing you that you would also likely fail at starting a business.

TAKING SMARTER RISKS

When I was in my twenties, I decided to pursue my dream of living at the beach in California. Having grown up in a fairly small town in the middle of Virginia, Los Angeles might as well have been the moon. I had no contacts there, no job prospects, and no idea how to find one (as much as I hate to admit it, this was several years before Facebook, LinkedIn, or Google). I wanted to pursue a career in advertising, and there was only one advertising agency within a two-hundred-mile radius of where I lived.

I had always imagined living in a bigger city—one with more culture, diversity, and opportunity. I had even begged my parents, at age thirteen, to please move the family to California. They very politely, and practically, declined to move cross-country simply because I liked the beach and wanted more excitement in my life.

Now, as an adult, I realized the decision was mine, and I decided to "go big." As far as big cities for advertising careers, the choices were obvious—New York or Los Angeles. I thought to myself, "Well, if I am going to be homeless, it is warmer in LA." My parents didn't find this particular criterion for the decision very encouraging.

But I didn't decide rashly; it was a calculated decision. I considered the options, counted up my savings, and made a plan. Friends and colleagues told me I was crazy and would never succeed. Bets were made regarding the number of days before I would come running back home defeated. I stopped asking people for their opinions—after all, none of them had ever lived in Los Angeles. As I made the decision, I focused on one question: "What's the worst that could happen?"

As it turned out, the worst was survivable. The absolute worst-case scenario was that I wouldn't find a job, and I would run out of money after three months. So, I made sure to set aside enough money to pay for four nights in cheap hotel rooms and enough gas to drive back across the country and beg my parents to sleep on their couch. Then, I gave away everything that didn't fit in my two-door car, including the house, and drove 2,650 miles to start over at twenty-seven.

I arrived in California, rented a temporary apartment, and slept on the floor because I didn't have enough money for furniture. In the first two months, I applied to over 150 jobs and had thirty-six interviews with no success. It was looking as though the worst-case scenario might apply. As my money was running low, I finally got an interview that paid off. I landed a great job with an international agency for double my previous salary. And, as a bonus, I was able to live at one of the most beautiful beaches in the world.

That move and that risk very literally changed my life, and it was eventually the catalyst to start my own successful business. The payoff was ten times greater than what I risked losing, but I would have never known if I had played it safe.

PUTTING RISK IN PERSPECTIVE

The secret to creating exceptional results is not to take bigger risks, but to reflect on your assumptions and ask tougher questions. Take time to check the accuracy of the shortcuts your brain might be using. This process will help you take smarter risks and use your energy and effort for the things that will bring the biggest and most meaningful rewards. When you take risks aligned with the results which are most important to you, the reward justifies the effort.

After interviewing dozens of people who have succeeded at a wide variety of goals in everything from business to sports and art, I find that most of them evaluate and approach risk differently.

They frame the risk and put things in a different perspective by asking tough questions and shifting their focus. Ironically, temporarily focusing on the worst-case scenario can improve the chances of success. This tactic makes something uncertain seem more real, and creates space to actively address the fears that otherwise block action. In addition, they find small ways to begin raising their awareness of the result they want. For example, someone who wants to start a business may join a co-working space for entrepreneurs. This one action can increase the availability of successful examples in their environment.

In my conversation with Christina, she described how she used some of these return-on-risk tactics in her approach to a big change. She was raised to be very responsible with money. It was important to her to never have any debt or be dependent on anyone else. For these reasons, she had always followed the traditional path in her education and career, or at least she attempted to. She had completed dual studies in college and had ambitiously set a goal to be at director level for an international company by age thirty.

She climbed successfully through her first steps in a corporate career. After several career moves, she started noticing a pattern. She realized that she loved the first six months at a job because of the new challenges, but then, she quickly became bored and frustrated. The corporate structure in the companies on her career path kept her from being creative and fully utilizing her skills and talents. She ran into roadblock after roadblock, being told that "It can't be done that way," or "We have to wait for approval."

Christina grew increasingly frustrated and got to the point where she barely had the mental energy to write a simple email. She was dragging herself through the day, and she knew she needed to make a change. At the same time, she didn't want to take a financial risk of starting something new without income. She tried making a safe change. She approached management and asked for a different role at her company, but after months of attempts, still had no success.

She recognized that perhaps her corporate career goals weren't aligned with her values of freedom and creativity, and she decided to take a different approach. She began taking writing courses to engage her creativity and found an opportunity to bartend on the side to earn extra money. She was working nine-to-five and then three days each week from 6 p.m. to 2 a.m. She enjoyed writing and wanted to start working as a copywriter, but her head was telling her she needed the money and security of a "real" job.

Finally, she calculated exactly how much she needed to cover her monthly bills and made sure she was earning that much at the bar. She quit her corporate job, and the hours at the bar gave her more time to work as a copywriter and pursue her dream. These incremental steps made the risk manageable. Only six months later, she had enough copywriting clients to replace her income and was able to quit the job at the bar.

I noticed that most people who have made an intentional and significant change have similar stories. They realize that something isn't working for them in the life they've designed, or that has been designed for them, and they start seeking a change. Then the fear of risking security, status, or reputation shows up and causes them to reconsider their decision. The common thread in how they move past this fear into taking action is that they put the risk into a different perspective by framing it with these three questions.

1) WHAT IS THE WORST THAT COULD HAPPEN IF I MAKE THIS CHOICE?

In Christina's case, the worst-case scenario was being financially dependent on someone else or needing to borrow money. When she asked herself this question, she realized that this was the fear keeping her stuck.

Most people find that even when they imagine the worst that can happen, it is manageable. It might involve sleeping on friends' couches or working at an odd job just to pay the bills, but it is usually survivable. Christina realized that even if she had no income, she could utilize her savings for a short time.

Often, overcoming the challenges that are most feared is the very experience that propels people to success.

2) HOW LIKELY IS THE WORST-CASE SCENARIO, REALISTICALLY?

Equally important to identifying the worst-case scenario is considering how realistic the chances are that it could happen. Our fears often blow things out of proportion to reality, and it causes paralysis. Stepping back to look objectively at the situation puts those fears in perspective.

For Christina, fear of not having any income at all was unrealistic. She knew she was qualified and capable of getting another job if she needed one, or that she was able to work at a variety of side jobs in order to pursue her goal.

Consciously recognizing the biases that impact our decisions when we try to solve complex problems too quickly allows us to find the flaws in the logic. Taking a more objective look, we usually see that the likelihood of the worst-case scenario is low.

3) WHAT CAN I DO TO REDUCE THE POSSIBILITY OF THE WORST-CASE SCENARIO?

This question is magic because it prompts planning to succeed and identifies many preventable risks. If the biggest threat is running out of money, is there a way to raise funds or reduce costs? If the biggest threat is unemployment, what could be done to put a safety net in place?

The process of asking these questions helps not only to improve the odds of success through better planning but also accomplishes the trick of putting your brain at ease, so that you can focus on the reward rather than the risk. Dedicating energy to actions that support the goal is a much more effective use of attention, rather than focusing on avoiding failure.

Everyone who has succeeded has also taken risks. The trick is not to avoid taking risks but to take smarter and more informed risks. Reduce the possibilities of failure and increase your chances of success. The saying "no risk, no reward" still applies.

Always playing it safe might eventually get you to your goals, but it will take a lot longer to get there. Being smart about the risks we choose to take gives us a much better chance at success. The people who achieve exceptional things tend to agree—the biggest risk is not taking one at all.

Even after you've decided to take a risk, it can be difficult to take the first steps and get into action. Next, we'll explore strategies you can use to start and sustain your momentum.

SUMMARY

- We evaluate personal risks by weighing the reward and relevance against the risk and opportunity cost.
- Biases can cause us to overestimate the risk, underestimate the reward, and seek information to support what we already believe.
- You can reframe risk and challenge these biases by asking these questions:
    - What is the worst that could happen?
    - How likely is the worst case, realistically?
    - What can I do to reduce the possibility of that result?
- Actively consider your Return on Risk to make smarter decisions about which risks are worth taking.

Clarity of Purpose

Overcome Expectations

Unapologetically Authentic

Return on Risk

Accelerate Action

Grow through Challenge

Embrace being Yourself

CHAPTER 9

REGAIN MOMENTUM

"I've been absolutely terrified every moment of my life—and I have never let it keep me from doing a single thing I wanted to do."

- GEORGIA O'KEEFFE

The most powerful lesson I have learned about how to overcome fear was completely accidental, at least for me. One sunny day in the Southern California desert, a simple conversation forever changed my perspective on fear.

I had always wanted to skydive. So, one Saturday afternoon, I drove a few hours away from Los Angeles into the desert for skydiving training and my first solo jump. I joined a group of about eight people in a classroom at the training center, and our instructor came in. I still recall the uncomfortable hush that washed over the room, as we immediately saw that he had only one leg. Our imaginations began sorting out which type of skydiving accident might have been the cause, and he had our complete attention for the safety training that followed.

Much later that day, I discovered that he lost his leg in a motorcycle accident only a few years earlier. That accident had forced him to change his career in his fifties. It was a low point in his life until he discovered his passion for skydiving. Since that time, he had made over two thousand jumps and had created a life where he got paid to do something he loved. The lesson he taught me later that day about fear still helps me with each new challenge in my life.

When we are faced with a new experience or some bold change that we've chosen to make, it is natural to feel some uncertainty. For our survival brain, uncertainty equals danger. If your brain doesn't know what to expect, it can't properly protect you. Uncertainty triggers our stress response, and we anticipate the worst. In fact, studies have shown that you are calmer anticipating pain than you are anticipating uncertainty, because at least the pain is certain.[93]

However, not much in life is certain. This is especially true as we are faced with making a change of some sort. In addition to the stress of the change itself, most of us compound the problem and create extra anxiety for ourselves in the form of doubt and worry. We overestimate the perceived threat and underestimate our ability to handle it.[94]

I find that this doubt and worry shows up in one of three specific ways. If you are an especially talented worrier, you might do all three.

1. Future Fear: Worrying about what might happen by focusing on all the things that could go wrong, but probably won't
2. Decision Doubt: Wondering "What the hell have I done?"
3. Rear-view Regret: Dwelling on how things were, looking backward, and longing for the past

The problem is that these use a lot of mental and emotional energy but don't move you any closer to your goal. Instead, they drain the energy you need to tackle the new challenge, leaving you weaker and less effective when you do finally move forward.

The best way to reduce the stress related to change and uncertainty is to start taking action. Even small actions make the

93 Bryan E. Robinson, Ph.D., "The Psychology of Uncertainty," *Psychology Today,* March 17, 2020.
94 Ibid.

situation feel more certain and create momentum that moves you forward. Fear holds us back from taking action. Recognizing the type of fear we create for ourselves can help to more easily overcome it.

FUTURE FEAR: "WHAT IF..."

My background is in the automotive industry, so I often use driving analogies. One of my favorite ways to illustrate how future fear keeps us from our goals is the fact that you can't steer a parked car. Even if you know where you want to go, the car must be in motion before you can turn right or left.

Let's say, you have an important meeting in part of the city where you don't normally drive. You wake up early, make yourself look fabulous, jot down the address, and go to your car. You get into the car and put the address into the navigation. But instead of putting the car in drive, you begin contemplating the "what ifs." "What if there is a traffic jam on that route? What if there is construction and the road is closed? What if the car breaks down, what if I miss the exit, what if I run out of gas..."

By now, you have been sitting in the car for ten minutes worrying about all the things that might happen, but aren't very likely, and you haven't gotten any closer to your destination. On top of that, you are now running late.

Any time you begin a thought with "what if," you are imagining something that might happen or might not. This takes your focus off of what you could do right now to get the result you want. When you look at it objectively, even if all those things happened, you would be perfectly capable of handling them. If there is a roadblock, you take a detour. If the car breaks down, you call for help. If you are low on gas, you stop and refuel. All solvable problems, but only possible to solve once you start moving. To ever have a chance of reaching your goal, you have to first step on the gas.

When we start something new or decide to take a risk, it is normal to feel some fear. Fear serves an important purpose in our lives. It is a built-in mechanism to protect us by triggering flight, fight, or freeze reactions.[95] Thousands of years ago, it kept us from getting eaten by tigers. Today, thankfully, most of us aren't faced very often with a fight for our lives. But our brain still has a similar reaction to threats, whether they are real or imagined.

As someone who has spent most of my career developing training to help people create new behaviors and adapt to change, I am familiar with the fears that even small changes can create. Instead of fear of death, our primary daily fears are now fear of failure, fear of not being good enough, or fear of making a mistake. The truth is, we often misuse fear in this context. Most often, we are actually experiencing anxiety, but we've integrated the concept into our vocabulary as fear.

People who achieved success by leading exceptional lives do not claim to be fearless. In fact, many of them easily

---

95 Kirsten Nunez, "Fight, Flight, Freeze: What this Response Means," *Healthline*, February 21, 2020.

describe points in their journey where they were almost paralyzed by fear. There were moments where they almost gave up. The difference is that they didn't stop the momentum. They kept moving toward their goals despite the fear that they felt.

My skydiving instructor was the person who helped me learn how it is possible to simultaneously acknowledge your fear and do the thing you are afraid of.

After he introduced himself to the class, he spent more than four hours explaining the most critical information for a solo jump. We learned about the correct form, how to open the parachute, and how to land. We also discussed what to do if the chute doesn't open, what happens if the chute is tangled, and what to do if you hit a tree or power line. Basically, we spent four hours on "what if," learning about all the things that could go wrong. Of course, the jump wasn't completely solo because you are accompanied by two instructors until the point your parachute opens. It is bad for business if students die on the first day.

We were all very nervous as we climbed into the plane and took off. The roar of the engines and the wind rushing past the open door made it impossible to have any conversation. This gave us fifteen minutes to sit and think (worry) about what was going to happen next. My heart rate climbed almost as quickly as the plane, and I watched the buildings below us become smaller and smaller. As we reached 12,500 feet in the sky above central California, we prepared to jump. When instructed, I walked up to the large open door of the airplane with an instructor on each side of me, anxiously rehearsing all the steps in my head. Above the noise, the instructor said, "Okay, we're going to jump on three." And he began the countdown, "one, two..." then suddenly I was plummeting through the air!

The adrenaline rush of the free fall and the sense of pure relief sixty seconds later, when I managed to open my chute properly, were breathtaking. The missing countdown number three was quickly forgotten.

The canopy flight drifting down slowly to the earth from 5,000 feet was one of the most amazing experiences I have ever had. It was simultaneously peaceful and exhilarating. I guided my chute easily and slowly back to the landing field and was ready to go again!

We had some time before the second jump, and I replayed the experience as I waited. Finally, curiosity got the best of me, and I asked our instructor to explain. "You said we were going to jump on three, but you only counted to two. What happened?"

He explained, after years of experience, they'd learned an important tactic. If they count to three, many students will panic and grab onto the airplane door at the last second. They hold on for dear life rather than jumping. Once they grab hold, there is almost no convincing them to make the jump. Fear wins.

Instead, the instructors don't allow the chance for fear to hold you back. They pull you out the door before your brain has had a chance to agree that you are ready.

Skydiving students make a decision to skydive, pay a significant amount of money, and invest hours in the lessons. It is something they want to do and have prepared for, but they still allow fear to stop them from achieving their goal. How often in our daily lives do we do exactly the same?

The truth is, no matter how much you prepare, you will never feel completely ready for a big leap.

Whether it is starting a business, changing careers, or any other big change, we make the decision and aim for our goal. We invest money in training and preparation. We learn how to avoid potential obstacles and make a plan for a smooth landing. We get ready to jump, and then stop ourselves from making the leap.

Why does this happen? For many people, it is because they don't feel ready *enough*. The "what ifs" begin to multiply and occupy their thoughts. The more they think about them, the more real they seem. "What if I missed something important in the instructions? What if I'm not smart enough, strong enough, or (fill in the blank) enough? What if, I fail?"

Fear still serves a purpose. It protects us from doing stupid things like jumping out of a perfectly good airplane. It is also the impetus to have a plan and a safety net or parachute. However, too often, we allow fear and worry to hold us back from the things we most want.

If we hesitate for too long, the fear prevails, and we miss out on what could possibly be the experience of a lifetime. The hardest part is starting. Once you take the first step, in spite of fear, it is easier to keep the momentum and navigate to your goal.

DECISION DOUBT: NOW WHAT?

Once you have made a decision and managed to take that first big leap toward your goal, it is exhilarating. You get excited about the possibilities and are ready to tackle the challenges... for about ten minutes. Then something really tricky happens. Your brain catches up and realizes what you have just done and slams on the brakes.

Many of the people I talked with, no matter how prepared, experienced this shortly after deciding on a big change. My colleague, Hannah, was no exception. Despite being successful, she was dissatisfied with her career and felt pulled toward bigger goals and adventures. With each day, she became increasingly restless and dissatisfied. She described feeling torn. Staying in her current situation would have been easy but unsatisfying. Making a change to pursue her dream would be difficult and risky.

Hannah's head and heart disagreed about what she should do. They had been battling it out for months in an ongoing dialogue that went something like this.

Head: I make a decent living and work close to home. I shouldn't be complaining; it could be so much worse. I'll just settle for a two-week vacation and learn to deal with the non-sense of this job better.

Heart: I want to be rid of the endless drama with my clients. I can't sit in these meetings anymore. It is killing my soul. I don't care about their products and all their problems that keep me awake at night. Why does this stress me out so much? I feel like I am losing my mind every day. I can't stop thinking about just quitting my job and going on a huge trip. Maybe I should take a huge "irresponsible risk" and go for it.

After months of wrestling with some version of this dialogue every day, Hannah finally chose to go for it. She decided to quit her job and travel for six weeks before finding her next career step. The risk of settling seemed greater than the risk of making a change. After making her decision, she felt a tremendous sense of relief. She gave her four-week notice at work, began planning her trip, and slept well for the first time in months.

The elation of her decision only lasted a few days. Then the doubt crept in, and Hannah started to question herself. She immediately began worrying about finding a new job, even though she clearly intended to take six weeks for traveling before starting the job search. She had enough savings to support this decision, but the doubt kept creeping back. She had made bold personal and career moves before, yet she was suddenly overwhelmed with uncertainty and doubts.

She recalls, "The questions and doubt suddenly crashed into my mind like a tsunami. I admit it, I was scared. There was no turning back. Soon I would no longer have a paycheck, and I would watch years of my hard-earned savings vanish."

As she transitioned from her current job, Hannah began to panic. Within days of making her decision, she started searching job boards and LinkedIn hoping for some reassurance that she would again find a way to pay her bills. She recalled previous job searches, with the hours and weeks of dedication and focus that were required. The more she thought about it, the more desperate she became. Instead of planning her amazing six-week trip through Spain and Portugal, she searched for a new job while still handing-off the current one.

Luckily, one day after hours scrolling through job posts with ever-increasing anxiety, Hannah recognized how her fear was sabotaging her plans and her excitement. She realized, "It was doing me no good. I was fast-forwarding into a time and place in the future that I didn't need to be in yet. I needed to stay present and stay focused."

Hannah reminded herself that she had planned to be out of work for a while. She had enough savings to cover it. She was a talented project manager and would certainly find a job again. She had a safety net. She took a deep breath and paused long enough to question how realistic her fears were. She realized that they were all manageable when it was time to deal with them, but that time was not now.

She refocused her attention on her immediate goal of traveling, rather than questioning her decision or worrying about what might happen months later. She stopped allowing worry about the future to distract her. Instead, she began the action she wanted to take—planning the trip of a lifetime.

Hannah did take her dream trip and, shortly after returning, landed a job much better suited for her. She even wrote a book, *Real Dreams, Real Advice,* to share her experiences and help others achieve their goals and dreams.[96] She says, "None of this would have happened if I'd let fears and doubts stand in the way."

REAR-VIEW REGRET

Sometimes, it is not worry about the future that causes us to doubt our decisions, but rather a sudden longing for the thing we just gave up. In talking to people about big changes in their lives, especially ones which they had actively chosen, I noticed a strange phenomenon. Almost every person had a moment where they not only doubted their decision but what they had chosen to give up also seemed much better than they originally thought.

You have probably noticed similar scenarios. As soon as someone commits to change something that makes them unhappy, they start to notice all the positive aspects. It often happens when someone finally ends a relationship after years of being miserable. Within a few weeks, they are crying on your shoulder about how wonderful their partner was and desperately plotting to win them back. Or someone starts a new job and can't stop talking about how fabulous

---

96 Hannah Welch, *Real Dreams, Real Advice: A Guide on Goal and Dream Achievement Based on Real Life Experience* (Los Angeles: Hannah Welch, 2014), Kindle.

everything was at their previous company. They start wondering, "What if I overreacted?" Suddenly the things that caused unhappiness in the previous situation seem small and insignificant, or forgotten completely, and the positive parts are magnified.

This scenario is caused in part by a type of decision regret which results from the way we relate to our goals. When we put our attention on a particular goal, like quitting a job or buying a new car, that goal becomes an active goal. "An active goal is simply one that has become energized by our motivational system." While the goal is active, things related to achieving it seem more valuable to us. [97]

In the case of quitting a job, for example, the goals of freedom and flexibility seem very attractive. However, once the goal has been achieved, it is no longer energized, and other goals get a new boost of energy and importance.[98] So, after quitting a job, the goals of security and status may suddenly take on new importance and cause you to regret the decision.

Of course, our fear of uncertainty can also play a role. When faced with something new, our brain comforts itself with the certainty of memories of the past. At least in that situation, we knew what to expect and how to cope. Even if the previous situation wasn't pleasant, the known undesirable scenario feels more comfortable than the unknown but more desirable possibility.

97 Art Markman, "Three Reasons Why You'll Probably Regret that Decision Later," *Fast Company,* September 12, 2016.
98 Ibid.

These two kinds of decision regret often have us wondering if we are crazy after making a big decision. Hannah's experience was no exception.

After she had quit her job, suddenly, Hannah began noticing all the things she liked about it. The clients were less annoying, she realized how much she liked her colleagues, and even the daily challenges of the job seemed less stressful.

She began to question herself: "What kind of crazy psychology is going on here? *Now* I think this is great? *Now* I like my job? *Now* I'm not stressed?"

This particular form of nostalgia can be crippling, as it keeps us wistfully looking backward through rose-colored glasses, rather than focusing our attention forward on our new goal.

The important point is to recognize it. Remind yourself of your goal and the values aligned with achieving it. Appreciate the fact that you can now also see the positive aspects of your previous situation and then remember why you wanted to change it.

You can't move forward by looking backward. Even if what you left behind you was good, there is a chance that what lies ahead of you can be great. Don't waste valuable energy looking behind you unless you want to go backward. Focus your attention and your energy on moving toward the possibilities that lie ahead of you and take action toward them.

Once you start moving, the momentum of each action will build on the next to accelerate your ability to succeed. You can use the strategies in the next chapter to create a mindset that makes it easier to sustain this momentum as you face new challenges.

SUMMARY

Our brain tries to protect us, whether the threat is real or imagined, holding us back from our goals in three ways:
- Future fear focuses time and energy on everything that could potentially go wrong.
- Decision doubt shows up shortly after making a decision, creating a cycle of worry and stress.
- Rear-view regret is looking backward and longing for the certainty of what we gave up.

Instead, use action, forward focus, and momentum to carry you in the direction of your goal
- Recognize that you are avoiding action with "what ifs"— start moving and steer as you go.
- Remember why you made the decision and refocus on your goal.
- Look forward to where you want to go, rather than backward to where you've been.

Clarity of Purpose

Overcome Expectations

Unapologetically Authentic

Return on Risk

Accelerate Action

Grow through Challenge

Embrace being Yourself

CHAPTER 10

REIMAGINE FAILURE

"Failure is simply the opportunity to begin again and this time more intelligently."

- HENRY FORD

Simone Giertz has created a job for herself, complete with a YouTube Channel and TEDx Talks, by building useless things. What is so special about these useless things is not actually the machines themselves but the mindset she uses to create them.

Simone had a problem many people have. She was afraid to fail and look stupid. Then she became interested in doing something very difficult—teaching herself how to build robots. Something that, according to her, "has a high likelihood of failure and moreover, has a high likelihood of making you look stupid."[99]

So how did she become successful at such a challenging goal when her performance anxiety was so strong? She came up with a way to succeed 100 percent of the time. She says, "instead of trying to succeed, I was going to try to build things that would fail." This new goal was smart in several ways. Not only was she learning, but she explains, "As soon as I removed all pressure and expectations from myself, that pressure quickly got replaced by enthusiasm."[100]

We have become conditioned to believe that failing at doing something means we ourselves are failures. Perhaps this mindset is more pervasive now because the expansion of technology allows our failures to be saved forever to the cloud, always threatening to resurface and embarrass us. Whatever the reason, many people try to avoid failure at all costs. But failing at a task and actually being a failure are two completely different

99   Simone Giertz, "Why You Should Make Useless Things," filmed April 2018 in Vancouver, BC, TED video, 11:50.
100 Ibid.

things. In fact, the incredibly successful people are often those that have failed the most, because they have also tried the most.

Simone figured out a unique way to turn failure into success. She gave herself permission to experiment and learn, and her enthusiasm grew. She redefined success, and it not only changed her results but also her motivation.

TWO POWERFUL WORDS

Failure serves an important function. It is how we learn new skills and improve current ones. It is often the most effective way to learn, as long as what you are learning is not skydiving. Think about it—no one ever learned to ride a bicycle by reading books or watching videos about bicycles. The only way to learn to ride a bicycle is by doing it. Of course, it is also valuable to have someone there to teach you or maybe add a set of training wheels. But, ultimately, you just have to get on the bike and start pedaling. Kids seem to know intuitively what many adults have forgotten—when you fall, get back up, dust yourself off, and try again. It is not the end of the world.

This same principle, which many successful people seem to grasp intuitively, can also be learned and applied by anyone. The concept is called growth mindset, and it comes down to two small words that can change your perspective and your performance.

Those two words are "not yet."[101]

---

101 *TEDx Talks*, "The Power of Yet, Carol Dweck," September 12, 2014, TED video, 11:18.

In her research with students in the United States, psychologist Carol Dweck showed how those two words could significantly impact performance. She observed that ten-year-old students initially had two very different reactions to being asked to solve a problem that was slightly too hard for them. When they were unable to solve the problem, many students saw it as a catastrophe. They felt as though they had failed.[102]

Other students, however, saw it as a chance to learn. They said things like, "I love a challenge," or "I was hoping this would be informative." Dweck describes this as the difference between a fixed mindset, the belief that intelligence and capability are fixed at a certain level, and a growth mindset, the belief that difficult challenges mean that I am learning.[103]

Dweck explored the impact of a growth mindset with groups of underperforming students in multiple schools. The students were taught that every time they push out of their comfort zone to do something difficult, the neurons in their brains form new, stronger connections, and over time, they can grow smarter. An incorrect answer was positioned not as a failure, but simply as "not yet" successful.[104]

By believing that every time they struggled, they were actually getting smarter, students embraced the challenges and saw failure as a chance to learn, rather than as an indicator of poor intelligence. With this new mindset for both students and

---

102 Ibid.
103 Ibid.
104 Ibid.

teachers, in less than twelve months the students who were previously failing outperformed top students across the country.[105]

The same principles can apply to doing anything new and challenging, whether it is work, sports or learning a new skill. Failure is a way to discover what doesn't work, so that you can try again with more information about how to succeed.

* * *

When I first began talking with Lynn Yap, I realized she was one of those people who just seemed to "get" this concept. She told me, "I am not comfortable when I am not learning. I am always looking for a new challenge." When I asked what she meant, she told me how after ten years building a life in New York she decided to start over again.

In 2014, Lynn was feeling restless. She had a successful career in investment banking in New York. She recalls the conversations she had then with friends and colleagues, all in their early thirties at the time. She explained, "We had done everything that we *'should'*—we had checked all the boxes—single, successful, working in finance in New York. Now what? Nobody said what comes next."

After a decade spent successfully building her career, she was left wondering, "What now?" She started working with a coach to get clarity on her goals. As a fun social activity, she and a few friends decided to get together one Friday night to drink some wine and create vision boards. These boards are

---

105 Ibid.

used as a sort of long-term goal-setting exercise. You pull pictures of things that inspire you from magazines or online and arrange them into a collage on a large poster board, which you then hang somewhere you can see daily. The pictures can be of anything—travel to exotic places, an executive office suite, a beautiful house, happy family, delicious food—whatever inspires you. Lynn and her friends had a lot of fun thinking about their vision for the future that spring evening, and she hung the board on her dining room wall.

About a month later, as Lynn was walking through the dining room, she noticed the board. A particular photo at the top left of the board caught her attention—old Victorian houses in a neighborhood in London. The picture sparked an idea, and she said out loud to herself, "I am moving to London."

Her decision wasn't quite as out of the blue as it seems. Lynn had also wanted to live in London years before when she completed her law degree there. At that time, she had applied to over one hundred law firms in two years, and she had received over one hundred rejections. It wasn't that she didn't have the right qualifications. The rationale she repeatedly received was that, because she was not from the UK, the firms were concerned that she would leave England and return to the US. The conservative hiring managers and partners weren't willing to take a risk on a "wild card." Even though Lynn had created a successful life and career in New York, her goal to work in London remained unfulfilled.

She decided it was time to pursue that goal. After realizing what she wanted to do, she acted quickly. The same evening, she told several friends of her plans. The next day at work, she told her manager. She explained to me, "If I tell it to the world, I have to do it. I announce it, and then I figure out how to do it." Now she was committed to the decision. She sold or gave away all of her things and planned her move across the Atlantic.

A short six weeks later, she arrived in London with two suitcases, no job, and only a ninety-day tourist visa. In the first two weeks, she began to panic a little bit. She gave herself a deadline of ten weeks to find a job. Otherwise, she would go back to New York.

She set ambitious targets and made a point to talk with at least two new people per day. These conversations helped her narrow down the types of companies and jobs that might be possible. However, the weeks slipped by quickly, and after dozens of conversations and applications, she wasn't any closer to finding a job. By early August, only a few weeks before her visa would expire, she had no leads. The complication of finding a company to sponsor a visa was bigger than she anticipated. It was now officially summer holidays, and hiring managers weren't even in the office.

She realized that she may fail to achieve her goal for reasons closely resembling those in her first attempt years earlier. She decided to let go of the pressure she was putting on herself. She told herself, "The most important thing was that I tried. I gave it my best and put in the effort, and that was more important than the end destination." Worst-case scenario, she would return to New York and find a job there. She made peace with the process and began to enjoy what she thought would be her last weeks in London. Then she received a reply from a start-up company willing to bring her on board as an interim COO.

This time, Lynn succeeded in her goal of working in London. Her previous attempt and the resulting career in New York had contributed to her ability to succeed. During that period, Lynn had changed industries and gained experience in an area that was much more transferrable, especially internationally. She had also gained confidence and connections, which gave her new leverage and strategies as she pursued her goal. She had been able to use the lessons learned from the initial attempt as a springboard to success rather than accepting it as a barrier, or worse, a signal that her goal wasn't achievable.

In my interviews, I struggled to find stories from people who had failed and then succeeded, which perplexed me. Finally, I realized that people who have a growth mindset don't think of it as failure, and, therefore, don't describe it that way. They talk about how much they enjoy a challenge, the lessons they learned, and the steps to achieving their goal. For them, a setback is not a failure but simply a part of the process and an opportunity to take a different approach.

You have only failed when you stop trying to reach the goal. When something doesn't go the way you hoped, just remember, it is not that you didn't succeed. It is that you haven't succeeded yet.

GROWTH IS UNCOMFORTABLE

Unlike Lynn, most of us usually resist or avoid situations that challenge us or make us uncomfortable. We hate our job, but we don't search for a new job because, after all, "it's not that bad." We don't have important, difficult conversations with our spouse/parents/friends because we don't want to create conflict. We don't try to learn new concepts that might change our perspective because that would mean we might be wrong about something. As a default, we seek security, comfort, and certainty. We want to know what to expect, what to do, and exactly how to succeed. We are very comfortable in our comfort zone.

Of course, as the saying goes, "The only things that are certain are death and taxes." So, whether we like it or not, the events of our lives are not certain, and we can't always know exactly what to do or what to expect.

What many people seem to have forgotten is that we only grow and improve when we are challenged by something that feels uncomfortable. Even something as simple as a fitness routine proves this point. While working toward a big deadline, I fell out of my normal exercise routine for a few months. After the project was finally completed, I was excited to return to the gym. The exercise felt great while I was there, but the next day, I could barely move. Everything hurt. Even putting on my shoes caused ripples of pain to shoot through my entire body.

Of course, most athletes know that muscle growth occurs only when the muscles are pushed beyond the point of comfort. Usually, this involves using more weight or more repetitions than the previous set. Some weightlifters intentionally train to the point of muscle "failure," when the muscle is no longer capable of lifting anymore. Pushing past the point of comfort, or even to failure, causes moderate damage or injury to the muscle fibers, which then grow and strengthen as the body repairs them.[106]

You've heard the saying "What doesn't kill you makes you stronger." It turns out, this is not only true when it relates to physical challenges, but also mental and emotional challenges.

Many people get so caught up in not wanting to feel uncomfortable or disappointed that they stop taking chances. They avoid anything that might cause a negative experience or emotion, but this avoidance can actually hold them back from leading fulfilling lives.

In her TEDx Talk on Emotional Agility, psychologist Susan David refers to this desire to avoid negative feelings as "having dead people's goals." She goes on to explain, "Only dead people never get stressed, never get broken hearts, never experience the disappointment that comes with failure[...] Discomfort is the price of admission to a meaningful life."[107]

In 2011, I certainly had enough discomfort in my life to create my fair share of negative feelings. My marriage was falling apart. Due to some naive decisions I made at the beginning of the relationship, getting divorced meant losing most of my savings. And, in order to protect the successful business I'd built from being torn apart in divorce negotiations, I would have to give it up as well.

---

106 Jayne Leonard, "How to Build Muscle with Exercise," *Medical News Today*, January 8, 2020.

107 Susan David, "The Gift and Power of Emotional Courage," filmed November 2017 in New Orleans, LA, TED video, 16:40.

I had been miserable for years, and it affected my health, my work, and my friendships. I knew I needed to make a change, but I had trouble letting go of an otherwise safe and comfortable life. I had a nice house, a successful business, and enough income to regularly travel, as well as enjoy the wide variety of entertainment available in Los Angeles. My brain seemed convinced that "known" misery was better than "unknown" possibility, especially in my mid-forties. What if I tried to make a change and failed?

Instead of being on the path to something meaningful, I felt lost and directionless. I could stay stuck in an undesirable situation or give up everything I had worked for and start over. I struggled to find my next steps or to make any decision at all, so I started to work with a coach.

On a day when I felt particularly frustrated and stuck, my coach told me the parable of the trapezes. She explained, the major events in our lives are like a series of trapezes. We swing comfortably on one, and it is easy to stay there gently rocking back and forth. Eventually, we see a new trapeze bar swinging toward us, and we know it is where we need to be. The problem—we can't reach out and grab the new trapeze bar without completely letting go of the safety and comfort of the bar we are currently holding onto. Then the choice is ours. We can stay on the current trapeze and keep the experience we already have or choose to let go and reach for the next experience.

Her framing of the situation made the choice clear to me. If I wanted to reach the next stage of my life, I had to let go of what I was holding onto. It became riskier to "play it safe" and stay stuck in a life that made me unhappy than to take a chance on something new.

The goal is neither to avoid risk entirely nor to take unnecessary risks, but to thoughtfully choose the risks that move you toward your goals. What is important enough to you to take a chance? The time between letting go of the first trapeze bar and grabbing onto the second is definitely scary. There is a panic-inducing moment of freefall, where there is nothing to hold onto and no support. The complete lack of structure or stability is a feeling we aren't accustomed to and don't handle very well. The first impulse is to try to grab the bar again. The second impulse is to look down at where you could fall. But both of these impulses will actually sabotage your success. These instinctive reactions will stop your progress or cause you to fall.

The trick to reaching the second bar is to focus on it and only on it. Looking backward, or holding on too long to the first bar, pulls your momentum backward. You will not have the necessary energy to reach the target. Looking down pulls your attention to exactly what you don't want, and the fear can paralyze you.

It takes some courage, but the only way you can move forward and grab the next bar is to focus on what you want. Once you have it in your grasp, you have time to look back and appreciate the feat you have just accomplished. The elation of reaching your destination and floating securely above the ground that you were plummeting toward only seconds earlier is worth every moment of doubt you had to overcome. You will wonder why you didn't do it sooner.

In order to learn and grow, it is necessary to embrace challenges rather than avoid them. When faced with a new challenge, remember this—get comfortable being uncomfortable. Or at least see that risking failure also means giving yourself the space to learn and succeed.

Challenges help make us stronger and more capable, and occasional failures are simply part of that process. The key to success is to be smart about the challenges you choose, and when you fall, pick yourself up and try again.

SUMMARY

- Trying, and failing, is how we learn new skills and improve on current ones. No one succeeds without also having some failures.
- Growth mindset is the belief that when we are challenged, we are learning. Our intelligence and capability can grow.
- Growth is uncomfortable, like building muscles. Discomfort is a signal that you are making progress.
- Changing your perspective to one of "not yet" can powerfully change your performance.
- People who achieve exceptional goals view failure not as the end but as a step in the process toward success.

Clarity of Purpose

Overcome Expectations

Unapologetically Authentic

Return on Risk

Accelerate Action

Grow through Challenge

Embrace being Yourself

CHAPTER 11

REINVENT YOUR LIFE

---

*"It takes courage to grow up and turn
out to be who you really are."*

- E.E. CUMMINGS

I started this book with the theory that the fervent pursuit of everything that we think we *should* do to be happy and successful is exactly the thing that is making us miserable and burnt out. We have more access to information, more opportunities, and longer life spans than ever before, and yet we are less satisfied, more stressed, and less happy than a few decades ago.[108] Somehow, we have collectively bought into the notion that there is a proven formula for success and happiness, and it is killing us.

We are persuaded of this notion every day of our lives, from the moment we can first understand the words yes and no. Our parents tell us what we should eat, what we should wear, and what we should believe. We look to our friends or colleagues for cues about how we should behave and what we should think. The media tells us what kind of car we should drive, which phone to buy, and what success looks like.

We see the people that have the life we think we want, and we try to copy their path to success. Or we try to find a shortcut or a life hack to get there faster. Then we reach our target, and it is still not enough. We achieve our goal, exhausted and shattered, and then look around and wonder why we wanted it in the first place. Or despite our efforts, we don't reach our goal, and we convince ourselves the people who did had exceptional talent or luck. We resign ourselves to a life of admiring them from the couch while binge-watching the latest Netflix series and wishing our life could be different.

---

108 John F. Helliwell, Richard Layard and Jeffrey D. Sachs, *World Happiness Report 2019* (New York: Sustainable Development Solutions Network, 2019).

After making two bold moves in my life, I talked to people every day that told me how stuck or trapped they felt in their current situation. They described dreams of a new career, better relationship, or grand adventure, but their stories always ended the same. They felt that they could not do those things because those dreams were only possible after some prescribed series of life events in a certain order. Or they thought those options were only available to people unlike them. The reasons all sounded logical and responsible:

- "We can travel more after the kids are grown."
- "I can't change careers. I have a mortgage to pay."
- "I'll start a business after I save more money."

When I pointed to examples of people who had done the things they dreamed of, the response was often, "Those are the exceptions."

I felt compelled to write this book after hearing repeatedly the frustration of smart, talented, and inspiring people, who had basically resigned themselves to a life of "good enough." I knew that they were capable of having exactly what they wanted. Their goals were within their reach, but they couldn't see it. My career in corporate talent development had shown me firsthand the powerful potential each person has to reach their goals, and I wanted to find a way to help others unlock that potential for themselves.

I proposed that the people we consider exceptional are normal people that do something differently to get extraordinary results and that we all have the power to be exceptional.

After completing months of research and dozens of interviews, I realize that my theory was only partially correct. I discovered that everyone has the capability within themselves to be exceptional if that is the path they choose. Exceptional success does not depend on special skills, good fortune, or even doing the right things in the right order. In fact, in most cases, relying solely on any of those things is a recipe for failure.

The people we deem exceptional simply take a different approach. They manage to recognize, ignore, or defy many of the tricks our brains play on us in an attempt to make sense of the world, conserve our energy, and keep us safe. They are able to overcome sabotaging thought patterns and behaviors, which impact how they handle the pressures of the world around them and the results they get.

These tricky traps include, but are not limited to, our natural tendency to meet the expectations placed upon us and seek evidence that confirms what we already believe. Also among the traps is the tendency to perceive things which could benefit us as threats. Instead of embracing action toward them, our brain responds with stress or fear that actively holds us back. We are bad at telling the difference between a perceived threat and a real one, and we often miscalculate the real risk and our chances of success or failure.

We believe that our best chance at survival is to simply fit in and go along with the crowd in the proven, low-risk approach to life. These tendencies serve a purpose; they help us to survive. But by keeping us in our comfort zone, they prevent us from achieving what is possible and limit our ability to thrive.

The people we consider exceptional are all as different from each other in their approach to their goals as the word itself suggests. They come from all backgrounds, cultures, socio-economic statuses, levels of education, and personality types. They are introverts and extroverts, scientists and artists, young and old. They are as diverse as the population in general. According to their own evaluations of themselves, they are not especially talented, lucky, or brilliant. In fact, the one thing that they all consistently share, at least the ones I researched, is that they all invested an incredible amount of time and effort in becoming great at what they do and achieving their goals.

Past that one commonality, they've taken different approaches, made different mistakes, and gotten different levels of results. There is no generic, one-size-fits-all formula to achieving exceptional success.

What I found is not that each of these people had a special gift. Instead, they had a specific kind of mindset and approach to life when pursuing their goals. What surprised me is that this mindset and approach is something that we are born with. Every single component of it are traits and behaviors that come naturally to us as children, but then most of us lose them somewhere between our terrible twos and our twenties. The people who lead exceptional lives have managed to hold onto these particular ways of approaching life, or they have rediscovered them after a long search.

This mindset and approach are what I have defined as a certain kind of courage. It is quite simply, the unwavering ability to be yourself and pursue your dreams, despite the pressure from the world around you to be something you are not.

THE COURAGE TO BE EXCEPTIONAL

It seems strange that it should take courage to be ourselves. But every day, we experience pressure from the people and world around us to conform to societal norms, expectations, and other people's definitions of how we should behave. We are so slowly immersed and indoctrinated into these norms that we don't even recognize it until we reach a point in our lives where it is so stifling that we begin to suffocate.

It is a bit like the fable of the boiling frog. As the fable goes, if you put a frog in a pot of cool water and then slowly increase the heat, the frog will not jump out because it becomes accustomed to the change in temperature slowly. Eventually, the frog will cook in the boiling water rather than leaping out to save itself. According to biologists, this is not actually correct, but the moral of the story is still widely used.[109] It is a metaphor for the inability or unwillingness of people to act when they have been slowly conditioned to particular situations or threats.

In my opinion, we have been slowly conditioned to accept a huge threat to our happiness and success—the pressure to be what we are told we *should* be. We don't notice it until it

---

109 Nick Obradovich and Frances C. Moore, "The Data is In. Frogs don't Boil, but We Might," *The Washington Post*, February 25, 2019.

is too late. The exceptions are the ones who dare to take the leap, buck the system, and jump out of the hot water that the rest of us are slowly boiling in. Or they were rebellious enough never to soak in it in the first place.

As I listened to stories from more and more people who had some version of this experience, my mood fluctuated wildly. At times, I became almost overwhelmed with the pressure our culture has created for us. But my excitement returned as I recognized that the potential for happiness is something that we all already have. We only have to find the power to recognize it and then choose to embrace it.

* * *

My journey in writing this book was, in many ways, an experiment in recognizing and testing for myself many of the concepts I was writing about. More than a few times, I found myself held back by the various *shoulds* dancing in my head, including the one saying that I should write the book following a certain formula. Even though my creative conscience screamed out against it, the pressure to follow standard templates and checklists was strong. I also noticed the stress and anxiety created by fear of taking the first big leap and announcing the book publicly. And then later, the resistance to risk as I found some very creative ways to procrastinate, rather than submit the first draft. With each step forward, I felt as though I was taking three steps backward.

Fortunately, due to the topic of the book, I was continually reminded of the strategies people used to overcome these challenges. I had a constant source of new energy as they shared the stories of powerful moments when they knew they had to do something differently. I looked at my own life and realized that there is still so much more that I have ahead of me. Writing this book was only the first step in pursuing my unique path. After more than two decades of a successful professional career, I am only at the beginning of my journey. Now, I can move forward with the confidence that it is possible to reach my destination, and I look forward to the lessons I will learn along the way.

It is not easy to make the leap into creating the life you want for yourself, but everyone I spoke with said it is absolutely worth it. Some took a slower, steadier approach, ensuring they had safety nets along the way. Others took an all-in approach and "built the plane as they were flying it." They all made mistakes, but none of them regretted the decision to pursue their own unique and unconventional path.

I hope that this book has helped you to see new perspectives and possibilities through real examples of people that have created phenomenal lives and impact from nothing other than their own drive, creativity, and sheer stubbornness. I intended to share the parts of the stories that are usually behind scenes yet contain some of the most important factors in contributing to the results. I wanted to show that we all face similar fears, challenges, and biases in judgment which have the power to hold us back from happiness. We can give into them, but I hope that by recognizing them in our daily lives, we can more easily overcome them to pursue our goals and achieve our own definition of success.

Which, in the end, is the only definition that really matters.

SUMMARY

- The pressure to be what the world tells us we *should* be is huge threat to our happiness and success.
- We all have the potential to lead exceptional lives, if we do things differently and have the courage to be ourselves.
- This courage comes naturally to us as children, but we lose it as we grow and give in to the pressures of the world around us to be something else.
- You can rediscover the courage to overcome expectations, pursue your own definition of success, and create the life you want.

CONCLUSION

There aren't many days of school that I remember clearly, but the final day of Ms. Breeden's English literature class is etched in my memory, and I think of it often. On this particular day, she wasn't teaching us literature. It was the last day of 8th grade, and we would soon be going onto high school and the bright futures that awaited us. She took her time that day to tell each student how much she enjoyed our individual contributions to the class.

As the class neared its final moments, she gave us this parting advice: "This above all to thine own self be true." Of course, she was quoting a verse from Shakespeare's *Hamlet,* but she said it with such heartfelt passion, it felt as if she was talking directly to me.

She knew then that each of her students had unique gifts to bring to the world, and she wanted us to believe it for ourselves. I never forgot her advice. Although I haven't always lived it, I have relied on those words in times when I struggled with choices of direction in my life. This book is in part a tribute to the confidence she gave me that day to pursue my dreams.

We are each exceptional. We lose sight of this quickly as we manage the stresses and pressures of daily life. It is easy to get caught up in the hype of everything we are told we *should* do, *should* want, and *should* be. But it is possible to choose a different path. This book is my attempt to tell the stories of people who have done that successfully, to remind us that it is possible to achieve our goals by being true to ourselves.

If you feel that you have lost yourself somewhere in the pace and pressure of daily life, these seven strategies can help you rediscover the courage to create the life you want.

1. **Clarity of purpose:** Don't settle for other people's definitions of success. Define your own goals aligned with your values and your dreams.
2. **Overcome expectations:** Be aware of whose expectations you accept. Don't get caught up in fulfilling expectations that are incorrect or misinformed. Rethink the expectations you have of yourself to create the results you want.
3. **Unapologetically authentic:** You are uniquely capable to be you, with all of your talents, strengths, and flaws. Don't waste valuable energy trying to hide your differences and be "normal." Stand out and be yourself.
4. **Return on risk:** Reconsider how you evaluate risks. Use strategies that help to reframe the uncertainty and focus on the rewards. Leading a low-risk life is the biggest risk of all.
5. **Accelerate action:** Don't let fear hold you back from your goals. Even small actions will move you closer to your goal. Build confidence, create momentum, and correct your course as you go, but get into action.

6. **Grow through challenge:** If you avoid challenges, you might avoid some failure, but you also miss out on success. Failure is not fatal or final. In fact, it is often the fastest way to grow through experience. Reframe failures as opportunities to learn and improve.

7. **Embrace being yourself:** Only you know how to lead the life that will make you happiest. Trust your instincts, embrace your quirks, and flaunt your fabulousness.

You have the power to choose the life you want to live. No one else can do it for you.

Have the courage to create the path that is right for you, move beyond *should,* and embrace being exceptional.

ACKNOWLEDGMENTS

I relied heavily on the collaboration and support of many people in the creation of this book. With each conversation, I gained new insights, inspiration and an increased awareness of the unlimited possibilities life offers us. I am grateful to everyone who helped me bring those ideas to life.

First, I'd like to thank everyone who took the time to share their stories, experiences and ideas: Alexandra Galviz, Amy Yip, Celesta Davis, Christina Brinkmann, Darrian Douglas, Hannah Welch, Helen Strong, Kristen Illes, Lynn Yap, Machiko Nagata, Marisa Keegan, Nikki Barua, Staci Taustine, Shelly Bouren, Sherri Durbin, Stacey Yip, and Victor Hailey

I am especially grateful to the people who offered their expertise and unending encouragement throughout the creation of this book:

- My editors: Whitney Jones, Mary Ann Tate, and Sarah Lobrot

- The friends and confidants who read early drafts, coached me through revisions and pushed me to make this book a reality: Matthias Riff, Shelley Randles, Talia Sherman, and Kathleen Zabaleta

And a special thanks to all the early supporters of the book:

Bob Ayoob, Karin Baeumler, Ashlee Berghoff, Jonathan Bravin, Anne Broudic, Kris Chandler Hastings, Kirsten Cherry, Carsten Cramer, Ivanna Cullinan, Claire Eby, Laurie Ellis, Susan Gawalt, Gillian Holmes, Andrea Hoymann, Kristen Illes, Navya Karnam, Marisa Keegan, Alex Langhans, Jeanne LeBlanc, Karolina Liszka, Kimberly Scata, Amy Maciejewski, Machiko Nagata, Andy Nijs, Ronald Oort, Shelley Randles, Matthias Riff, Mark Rogers, Brian Scheff, Talia Sherman, Jeff Spoeri, Brian Trainor, Sirah Vettese, Robin Walker, Jim Welch, Julieann Wolowicz, Michael Womack, Dorothy and Gilmer Womack, Lynn Yap, Stacey Yip, and Kathleen Zabaleta

Finally, I'd like to express my gratitude to my family for always supporting the crazy ideas that take me in new directions on my own path in life.

APPENDIX

INTRODUCTION:

Galviz, Alexandra (Authentic Alex). "When I was a little girl, I used to secretly dream of working in that really tall building with the pointy top..." LinkedIn, February, 2017. https://www.linkedin.com/feed/update/urn:li:activity:6639108553367924736/.

Helliwell, John F., Richard Layard and Jeffrey D. Sachs. *World Happiness Report 2019*. New York: Sustainable Development Solutions Network, 2019. https://worldhappiness.report/ed/2019/.

Leonard, Jayne. "How to Handle Impostor Syndrome." *Medical News Today*, September 29, 2020. https://www.medicalnewstoday.com/articles/321730.

Newman, Kira. "World Happiness Report Finds that People are Feeling Worse." *Greater Good Magazine*, March 20, 2019. https://greatergood.berkeley.edu/article/item/world_happiness_report_finds_that_people_are_feeling_worse.

Wigert, Ben, and Sangeeta Agrawal. "Employee Burnout, Part 1: The 5 Main Causes." *Gallup*, July 12, 2018. https://www.gallup.com/workplace/237059/employee-burnout-part-main-causes.aspx.

CHAPTER 1:

Canfield, Jack. "The Formula that Puts You in Control of Success." *Jack Canfield's Blog*. Accessed February 4, 2021. https://www.jackcanfield.com/blog/the-formula-that-puts-you-in-control-of-success/.

Colvin, Geoff. *Talent is Overrated: What Really Separates World-Class Performers from Everybody Else*. New York: Portfolio/Penguin, 2008. Kindle.

Dweck, Carol. *Mindset: The New Psychology of Success*. New York: Ballantine Books, 2016. Kindle.

Talks at Google. "The Growth Mindset: Carol Dweck." July 16, 2015. Video, 47:25. https://www.youtube.com/watch?v=-71zdXCMU6A .

CHAPTER 2:

APA Dictionary of Psychology. s.v. "heuristic (n.)" Accessed February 7, 2021. https://dictionary.apa.org/heuristic.

Berdick, Chris. *Mind Over Mind: The Surprising Power of Expectations*. New York: Penguin, 2012. Kindle.

Bubic, Andreja et al. "Prediction, Cognition and the Brain." *Frontiers in Human Neuroscience*, vol. 4 25. (March 22, 2010). https://doi.org/10.3389/fnhum.2010.00025.

Cambridge Dictionary. s.v. "cognitive bias (n.)" Accessed February 28, 2021. https://dictionary.cambridge.org/dictionary/english/cognitive-bias.

Cohen-Sandler, Roni. *Stressed Out Girls: Helping Them Thrive in the Age of Pressure.* New York: Viking / Penguin Group, 2006.

Encyclopedia Britannica Online. s.v. "Self-fulfilling prophecy." August 1, 2016. https://www.britannica.com/topic/self-fulfilling-prophecy.

Encyclopedia Britannica Online. s.v. "Confirmation bias." October 9, 2019. https://www.britannica.com/topic/confirmation-bias.

Merriam-Webster. s.v. "expect (v.)" Accessed February 4, 2021. https://www.merriam-webster.com/dictionary/expect.

Miller, R. L., P. Brickman, and D. Bolen. "Attribution versus Persuasion as a Means for Modifying behavior." *J Pers Soc Psychol.* no. 31(3) (March 1975):430-41. doi: 10.1037/h0076539. PMID: 1151610.

Rosenthal, R. and K. L. Fode. "The Effect of Experimenter Bias on the Performance of the Albino Rat." *Behavioral Science, 8*(3), 183–189. doi: 10.1002/bs.3830080302.

Skybrary. "Flight Crew Expectation Bias." Last modified September 4, 2019 at 9:10. https://www.skybrary.aero/index.php/Flight_Crew_Expectation_Bias.

CHAPTER 3:

Cherry, Kendra. "The 5 Levels of Maslow's Hierarchy of Needs." *Verywell Mind.* June 3, 2020. https://www.verywellmind.com/what-is-maslows-hierarchy-of-needs-4136760.

Gough, Christina. "Health and Fitness Clubs Statistics & Facts." Statista. Nov. 16, 2020. https://www.statista.com/topics/1141/health-and-fitness-clubs/.

Horney, Karen. *Neurosis and Human Growth: The Struggle Toward Self-Realization.* New York: W. W. Norton & Company, Inc., (1950) 1991 edition.

Maslow, Abraham H. "A Theory of Human Motivation." *Psychological Review 50*, no. 4 (1943): 370–396. https://doi.org/10.1037/h0054346.

Mulvey, Kelsey. "80% of New Year's Resolutions Fail by February - Here's How to Keep Yours." *Business Insider,* January 4, 2017. https://www.businessinsider.com/new-years-resolutions-courses-2016-12?r=DE&IR=T.

RSA. "RSA Replay: Emotional Agility." April 7, 2016. Video, 58:24. https://youtu.be/VM5V6_CkYCo.

World Health Organization. "Obesity and Overweight." April 1, 2020. https://www.who.int/news-room/fact-sheets/detail/obesity-and-overweight.

CHAPTER 4:

Brown, Brené. "The Power of Vulnerability." Filmed June 2010 in Houston, TX. TED Video, 20:04. https://www.ted.com/talks/brene_brown_the_power_of_vulnerability.

Helliwell, John F., Richard Layard and Jeffrey D. Sachs. *World Happiness Report 2019.* New York: Sustainable Development Solutions Network, 2019. https://worldhappiness.report/ed/2019/.

"The Mental and Physical Well-Being of Incoming Freshmen: Three Decades of Research." *Higher Education Today,* September 6, 2018. https://www.higheredtoday.org/2018/09/06/mental-physical-well-incoming-freshmen-three-decades-research/.

CHAPTER 5:

Iny, Danny. "What Science Says About Going Outside Your Comfort Zone." *Inc.,* November 8, 2016. https://www.inc.com/danny-iny/what-science-says-about-going-outside-your-comfort-zone.html.

CHAPTER 6:

Anthony, Scott D. "Kodak's Downfall wasn't about Technology." *Harvard Business Review,* July 15, 2016. https://hbr.org/2016/07/kodaks-downfall-wasnt-about-technology.

Barua, Nikki and Kara Goldin. "Episode 104: Overcoming Doubts and Doubters with Hint CEO Kara Goldin." October 21, 2020. In *Beyond Barriers.* Podcast, audio, 42:46. https://www.iambeyondbarriers.com/blog/overcoming-doubts-and-doubters-with-hint-ceo-kara-goldin.

Business Insider. "The Rise and Fall of Blockbuster and How It's Surviving with Just One Store Left." August 12, 2020. Video, 08:27. https://www.businessinsider.com/the-rise-and-fall-of-blockbuster-video-streaming-2020-1?r=DE&IR=T.

Goldin, Kara. *Undaunted: Overcoming Doubts and Doubters.* New York: HarperCollins Leadership, October 2020. Kindle.

Google: News from Google. "Larry Page's University of Michigan Commencement Address." May 2, 2009. Video, 16:28. http://googlepress.blogspot.com/2009/05/larry-pages-university-of-michigan.html.

Grant, Adam. "WorkLife with Adam Grant: The Creative Power of Misfits." March 2019. TED podcast, audio, 40:17. https://www.ted.com/talks/worklife_with_adam_grant_the_creative_power_of_misfits/transcript?language=en&referrer=playlist-worklife_with_adam_grant_mar_2019#t-2441.

Kara Goldin. "My Story." Accessed February 12, 2021. https://karagoldin.com/my-story.

Kloss, Kelsey. "The Magical Moment Your Pre-schooler Starts Coloring Inside the Lines." *Scholastic,* December 14, 2018. https://www.scholastic.com/parents/books-and-reading/raise-a-reader-blog/developmental-milestones-coloring-in-the-lines.html.

CHAPTER 7:
Biography. "Will Smith Biography." Updated January 8, 2021. Accessed March 2, 2021. https://www.biography.com/actor/will-smith.

Hunt, Vivian et al. *Delivering through Diversity*. McKinsey & Company, 2018.

Jean-Baptiste, Annie and Monica Marquez. "Episode 69: How Your Authenticity Fuels Innovation with Google's Annie Jean-Baptiste." in *Beyond Barriers*. Podcast, audio, 35:57. https://www. iambeyondbarriers.com/blog/how-your-authenticity-fuels-innovation-with-google-s-annie-jean-baptiste.

Lanier, Heather. "Good and Bad are Incomplete Stories We Tell Ourselves." Filmed October 2017 at TED Institute in partnership with BCG, Milan, Italy. Video, 13:28. https://www.ted.com/talks/heather_lanier_good_and_bad_are_incomplete_stories_we_tell_ourselves.

Page, Scott E. *The Diversity Bonus: How Great Teams Pay Off in the Knowledge Economy*. New Jersey: Princeton University Press, 2017.

Stagge, Nick and Nikki Barua. "This is Nikki Barua." in *The Ordinary*. April 29, 2020. Podcast, audio, 53:57. https://anchor.fm/theordinary/episodes/This-is-Nikki-Barua-eddjv7.

The Numbers. "The Numbers Bankability Index." Accessed March 2, 2021. https://www.the-numbers.com/bankability.

W Magazine. Murphy, Eddie. "Eddie Murphy on the Worst Advice He Received." January 20, 2020. Video, 4:38. https://www.youtube.com/watch?v=RWDSD41Xw3E.

Wiltons, Rebbekah. "The Fascinating Life Story of Will Smith." *Worldation* (blog). October 16, 2018. https://worldation. com/stories/the-fascinating-life-story-of-will-smith/.

CHAPTER 8:

Buzzfeed. "The Chances of You Being Famous," February 11, 2014. Video, 1:49. https://www.buzzfeed.com/dimitri/the-chances-of-you-being-famous.

Centers for Disease Control and Prevention. "Lightning: Victim Data." Accessed February 12, 2021. https://www.cdc.gov/disasters/lightning/victimdata.html.

Cherry, Kendra. "What is Cognitive Bias," *Verywell Mind.* July 19, 2020. https://www.verywellmind.com/what-is-a-cognitive-bias-2794963.

Encyclopedia Britannica Online, s.v. "Confirmation Bias." October 9, 2019. https://www.britannica.com/science/confirmation-bias.

"In Pictures: The Greatest Risk They Ever Took: James Dyson," Interviewed by Matthew Kirdahy in 2008. *Forbes.* January 21, 2010. https://www.forbes.com/2010/01/20/gucci-indy500-letterman-entreprenuer-management-risk-greatest_slide.html#52fc204325aa.

Kahneman, Daniel. *Thinking, Fast and Slow.* London: Penguin Random House, 2012.

New York State Lottery. "Odds and Prizes." Accessed February 12, 2021. https://nylottery.ny.gov/draw-game?game=powerball#odds_prizes.

Ocker, Lisa. "Business Branson Style." *Success* (blog). April 30, 2008. https://www.success.com/business-branson-style/.

"Slip and Fall Accident Stats." Lawfirms.com. Accessed February 12, 2021. https://www.lawfirms.com/resources/personal-injury/slip-and-fall-accident/slip-and-fall-accidents.htm.

Year On (blog)."Failure. Rejection. Success: The J.K. Rowling Story." January 15, 2015. Accessed February 12, 2021. https://www.yearon.com/blog/jk-rowling-failure.

CHAPTER 9:

Markman, Art. "Three Reasons Why You'll Probably Regret that Decision Later." *Fast Company*. September 12, 2016. https://www.fastcompany.com/3063598/three-reasons-why-youll-probably-regret-that-decision-later.

Nunez, Kirsten. "Fight, Flight, Freeze: What this Response Means." *Healthline*. February 21, 2020. https://www.healthline.com/health/mental-health/fight-flight-freeze.

Robinson, Bryan E. Ph.D. "The Psychology of Uncertainty." *Psychology Today*. March 17, 2020. https://www.psychologytoday.com/us/blog/the-right-mindset/202003/the-psychology-un-certainty.

Welch, Hannah. *Real Dreams, Real Advice: A Guide on Goal and Dream Achievement Based on Real Life Experience*. Los Angeles: Hannah Welch, 2014. Kindle.

CHAPTER 10:

David, Susan. "The Gift and Power of Emotional Courage." Filmed November 2017 in New Orleans, LA. TED video, 16:40. https://www.ted.com/talks/susan_david_the_gift_and_power_of_emotional_courage.

Giertz, Simone. "Why You Should Make Useless Things." Filmed April 2018 in Vancouver, BC. TED video, 11:50. https://www.ted.com/talks/simone_giertz_why_you_should_make_useless_things.

Leonard, Jayne. "How to Build Muscle with Exercise." *Medical News Today.* January 8, 2020. https://www.medicalnewstoday.com/articles/319151#how-does-muscle-grow-in-the-body.

TEDx Talks. "The Power of Yet |Carol Dweck." September 12, 2014. Video, 11:18. https://www.youtube.com/watch?v=J-swZaKN2Ic.

CHAPTER 11:

Helliwell, John F., Richard Layard and Jeffrey D. Sachs. *World Happiness Report 2019.* New York: Sustainable Development Solutions Network, 2019. https://worldhappiness.report/ed/2019/.

Obradovich, Nick and Frances C. Moore. "The Data Is in. Frogs don't Boil, but We Might." *The Washington Post,* February 25, 2019. https://www.washingtonpost.com/weather/2019/02/25/data-are-frogs-dont-boil-we-might/.

Made in United States
Orlando, FL
14 July 2023

35144409R00114